The Grand Palace

Naengnoi Suksri
Photography Michael Freeman

The Emerald Buddha Temple is surrounded by high, white-washed walls. Two of the eight prangs which are situated outside the cloisters can be clearly seen.

RIVER BOOKS GUIDES

The Grand Palace

Naengnoi Suksri
Photography Michael Freeman

RIVER BOOKS

River Books is deeply honoured and grateful that
His Majesty the King graciously permitted photography in
many areas of the Grand Palace not normally accessible.

First published in 1998 by
River Books, 396/1 Maharaj Rd, Tatien, Bangkok 10200
Tel: (66 2) 224-6686, 225-0139, 225-4963
Fax: (66 2) 225-3861, E-mail: riverps@ksc.th.com
Revised edition printed in 2000

British Library Cataloguing-in-Publication Data.
A catalogue record for this book is available from the British Library.

ISBN: 974 8225 48 8

English translation and additional material
Narisa Chakrabongse

Editor Narisa Chakrabongse
Design Supadee Ruangsakvichit
Production Paisarn Piemmettawat

Colour Separation by 71 Interscan.
Printed and bound in Thailand by Amarin Publishing and Printing (Public) Co., Ltd.

Contents

The approximate English translation of the building name is given in brackets where appropriate.
Numbers after the name relate to the plans.

Introduction

The highlight of any visit to Bangkok is a trip to the Grand Palace, which is the 'jewel in the crown' of Bangkok and represents the finest flowering of Rattanakosin art and culture. Begun by King Rama I, the Grand Palace has been extensively modified and remodelled during subsequent reigns and is thus a storehouse of Thai architectural and decorative style over the last two hundred years. In addition, at certain periods other influences predominate such as the Chinese elements, or the Western touches and building styles introduced by certain kings. Aiming to recreate the glory of the vanquished capital city of Ayutthaya, all the kings of the Chakri dynasty have lavished attention and care on its beautification and maintenance.

During the period of Absolute Monarchy which lasted until 1932, the Grand Palace was both the administrative and religious centre of the kingdom, as well as the residence of the king and the royal family, and, accordingly, required the construction of many magnificent throne halls, residential palaces and administrative offices, while the Emerald Buddha Temple complex was built to enshrine the venerated Emerald Buddha, the Palladium of State.

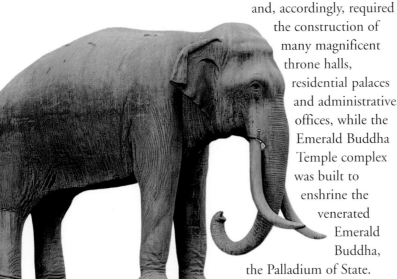

Above: The emblem of the Chakri dynasty.

Left: One of the pair of bronze elephants flanking the steps on the Phra Thinang Chakri Maha Prasat.

Opposite: Looking through the Phiman Chai Sri Gate to Phra Thinang Chakri Maha Prasat.

Above: The throne within Phra Thinang Amarin Winichai during a royal ceremony, c. late 1920s. (RBC)

Top: The end of Ratchadamnoen Avenue looking south toward Sanam Luang with the Grand Palace in the background c. 1910. (RBC)

The Grand Palace may thus be envisaged as a city within a city, whose huge white-washed castellated walls with walkways and battlements for guards, mirrored the walls and forts of Bangkok itself. Until the 1920s the Grand Palace remained the principal residence of the king, the royal family and the royal household. The inhabitants numbered many hundreds and for this reason a special set of rules were drawn up to govern behaviour. Indeed, at one time, there was even a small stronghouse for those who enfringed these rules.

Every aspect of its architecture is laden with religious and royal symbolism, all with the aim of conveying the sacred nature and power of the king. The special architectural vocabulary and iconography employed since the time of Ayutthaya to enhance royal buildings was continued and developed here, and expensive materials were used throughout. The buildings are resplendent with glittering gold which adorns the soaring spires of the palaces and the *chedi* (stupas housing relics), while the brightly-coloured porcelain tiles of the roofs, the abundant use of glass mosaic of differing colours and the carved and gilded pediments contribute to the impression of richness and vibrancy. Around the principal buildings are many small shrines, Chinese statues, small gardens and other unusual figures to intrigue the visitor and enhance the beauty of the whole.

Opposite: One of the garudas *holding* nagas *which were placed at the four corners of the base of the spire on Dusit Maha Prasat.*

A panoramic view of the Grand Palace looking west, showing the Chao Phraya River behind.

Right: Plan of the area around the Grand Palace.

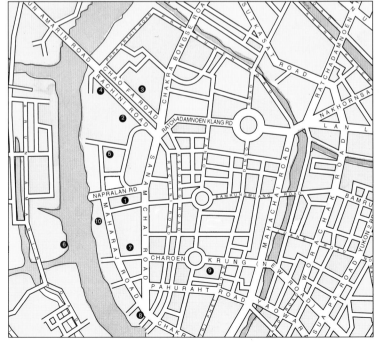

1 Grand Palace, 2 National Museum, 3 National Gallery, 4 National Theatre, 5 Wat Mahathat,
6 Wat Arun, 7 Wat Pho, 8 Flower Market, 9 Chinatown, 10 Boat pier to Wat Arun

Location and History

The Grand Palace is situated on a rectangular piece of land between Wat Pho and Wat Mahathat *(see plan)*. The site was originally occupied by a Chinese community, whom King Rama I (r.1782-1809) had transferred to an area outside and to the south of the city walls, the area known today as Chinatown.

Only 15 years after the disastrous second sack of Ayutthaya by the Burmese in 1767, King Rama I was determined to recreate the glory of the city that had been Thailand's capital for over 400 years, and ordered that construction of the palace should begin on 6 May, 1782. At first a temporary royal residence made of wood was surrounded by a simple log pallisade. Then on 10 June the king ceremonially crossed from the Thonburi side of the river to reside in his new palace as well as installing himself as the first king of the Chakri dynasty. Following these ceremonies the king began rebuilding the structures in masonry and added the forts, gates and throne halls, royal residences and, importantly, the palace chapel, which would occupy the same position as Wat Phra Sri Sanphet in Ayutthaya and would house the Emerald Buddha. After completion of the palace, the full traditional coronation ceremony was held in 1785.

The Emerald Buddha in Hot Season robes.

Below Left: His Majesty King Bhumibol Adulyadej cleaning the Emerald Buddha before changing his raiment.

Below Right: His Majesty wringing out the cloth used to wash the Emerald Buddha in order to collect the water. HRH Princess Maha Chakri Sirindhorn looks on at right.

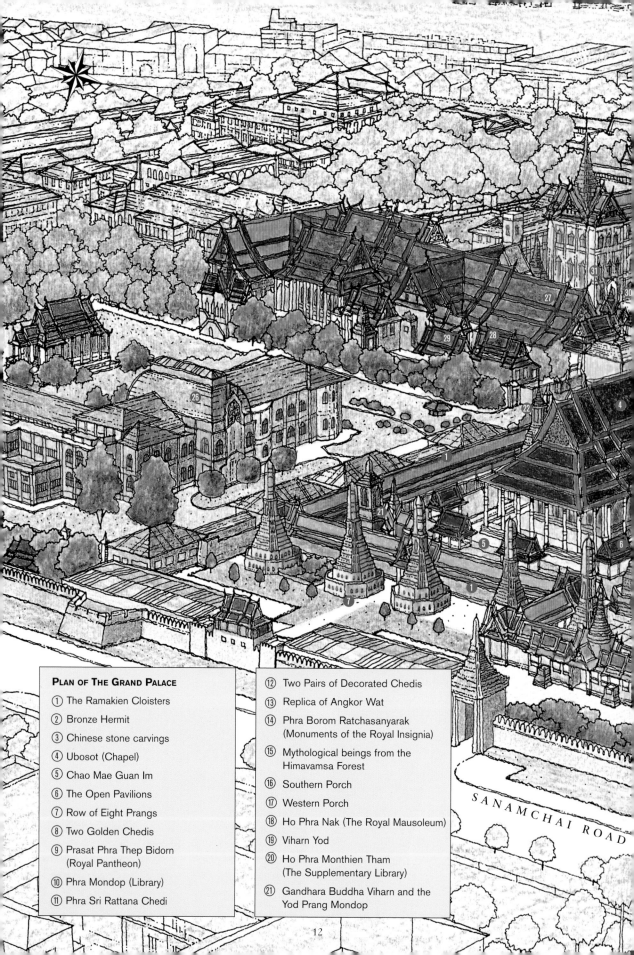

PLAN OF THE GRAND PALACE

1. The Ramakien Cloisters
2. Bronze Hermit
3. Chinese stone carvings
4. Ubosot (Chapel)
5. Chao Mae Guan Im
6. The Open Pavilions
7. Row of Eight Prangs
8. Two Golden Chedis
9. Prasat Phra Thep Bidorn
   (Royal Pantheon)
10. Phra Mondop (Library)
11. Phra Sri Rattana Chedi
12. Two Pairs of Decorated Chedis
13. Replica of Angkor Wat
14. Phra Borom Ratchasanyarak
    (Monuments of the Royal Insignia)
15. Mythological beings from the
    Himavamsa Forest
16. Southern Porch
17. Western Porch
18. Ho Phra Nak (The Royal Mausoleum)
19. Viharn Yod
20. Ho Phra Monthien Tham
    (The Supplementary Library)
21. Gandhara Buddha Viharn and the
    Yod Prang Mondop

SANAMCHAI ROAD

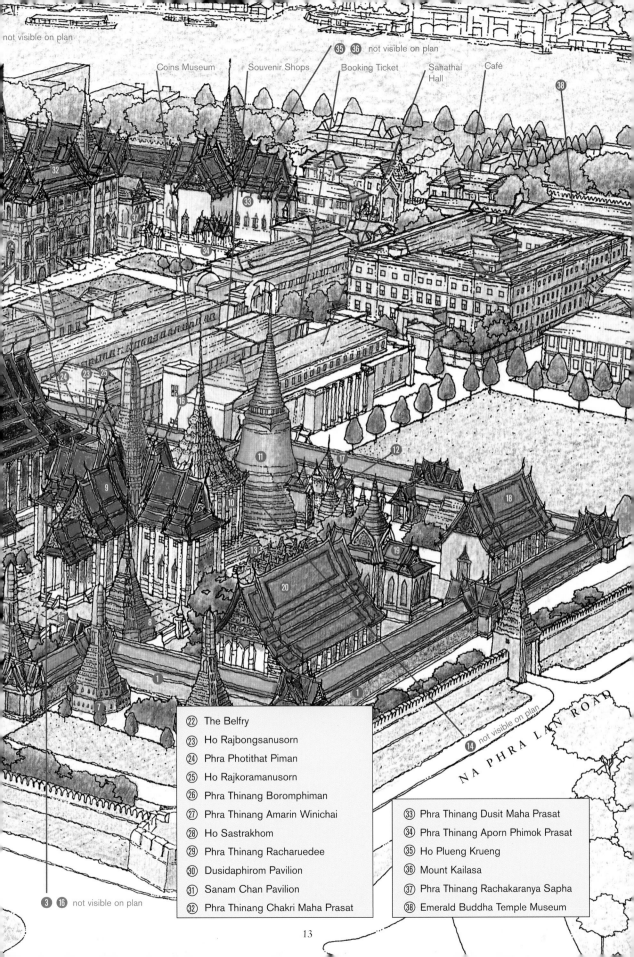

not visible on plan

㉟ ㊱ not visible on plan

Coins Museum Souvenir Shops Booking Ticket Sahathai Hall Café

32

37

33

34

㉟ ㊱

24 23 25

16

38

9

11

17

12

10

18

13

15

19

8

20

1

7

1

14 not visible on plan

N A   P H R A   L A N   R O A D

㉒ The Belfry
㉓ Ho Rajbongsanusorn
㉔ Phra Photithat Piman
㉕ Ho Rajkoramanusorn
㉖ Phra Thinang Boromphiman
㉗ Phra Thinang Amarin Winichai
㉘ Ho Sastrakhom
㉙ Phra Thinang Racharuedee
㉚ Dusidaphirom Pavilion
㉛ Sanam Chan Pavilion
㉜ Phra Thinang Chakri Maha Prasat

㉝ Phra Thinang Dusit Maha Prasat
㉞ Phra Thinang Aporn Phimok Prasat
㉟ Ho Plueng Krueng
㊱ Mount Kailasa
㊲ Phra Thinang Rachakaranya Sapha
㊳ Emerald Buddha Temple Museum

③ ⑯ not visible on plan

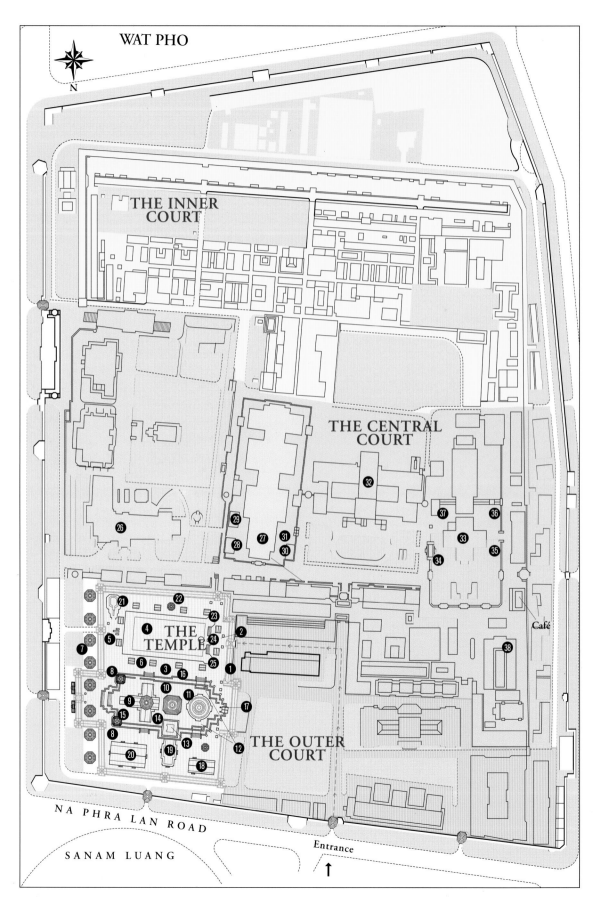

WAT PHO

N

THE INNER
COURT

THE CENTRAL
COURT

THE TEMPLE

THE OUTER
COURT

Café

NA PHRA LAN ROAD

SANAM LUANG

Entrance

14

Plan of the Grand Palace

The plan of the Grand Palace followed that of the royal palace of Ayutthaya, both in the choice of a comparable location and in its division into separate parts. Thus it was situated on the river bank facing north, with the river to the west and a road to the east. The city walls by the river functioned as the palace walls and the Temple of the Emeral Buddha as the royal chapel. The architecture, size, plan, and sites of the throne halls and royal residences corresponded to those of the royal palace at Ayutthaya, as did the forts and gates around the walls of the palace and the house on piles on the river bank that served as a landing stage for the King when he travelled by barge.

Above: King Rama I, founder of the Chakri Dynasty.

Left: Panoramic view of the Grand Palace looking west, photographed in the 1900s. Preparations were taking place for a cremation on Sanam Luang ground. The Temple of the Emerald Buddha is clearly visible, with the spire of the Temple of the Dawn just discernible in the background. (RBC)

Opposite: Plan of the Grand Palace showing its division into four main areas. The key to the numbers is on pages 12-13. The numbers remain constant through out the book.

Cast iron decoration above the doorway to Phra Thinang Chakri.

Above right: Panoramic view at night of the Grand Palace showing the Emerald Buddha Temple.

To the north of the Grand Palace, there was a large field known as Sanam Luang, as there had been in Ayutthaya, and a path leading to the Front Palace – *Wang Na*. (In the early reigns of the Chakri Dynasty, the prince of the *Wang Na* served as a kind of Deputy King or Viceroy). This open site was used for royal ceremonies and as a parade ground. In the east there was another field called Sanam Chai. Towards the southern end of the eastern wall there was a pavilion named Sutthaisawan Prasat, which served as a royal reviewing stand from where the king might view processions, or have monks sprinkle holy water upon those taking part.

During the reign of King Rama II (r.1809-1824), the palace compound and its walls were extended towards the south by moving the palace officials elsewhere. The gun emplacements on the walls were replaced with guard houses for those on duty and these were giving rhyming names. After this time, the compound was not further enlarged. Currently the Grand Palace covers an area of 152 rai, equivalent to 61 acres, or 218,400 square metres. The northern wall measures 410 metres, the east 510 metres, the south 360 metres and the west 630 metres, making a total of 1910 metres. The six octagonal towers date from the reign of King Rama I, while the three square towers date from the reign of King Rama II.

The compound of the Grand Palace was divided into four parts: *(see plan on p.14):* the Outer Court, the Central Court, the Inner

Court, and the compound of the Temple of the Emerald Buddha, each clearly defined with respect to function and the people who lived and worked there. The areas that both males and females and primces before thier tonsulate were allowed to enter were bounded by buildings or walls. The Inner Court, often referred to as the Inside, where only females and princes before their tonsurate were permitted, was enclosed by a high, massive wall and female guards stood at the entrances to this compound. Areas requiring high security had outer as well as inner doors of immense weight and size.

The Outer Court was situated in the front part of the Grand Palace to the north. Here were located the government departments in whose duties the king was directly involved, such as the Sala Lukkhunnai, the headquarters of the ministers of civil

The Central Court of the Grand Palace, looking towards Phra Thinang Chakri Maha Prasat with Phra Thinang Aporn Phimok Prasat in the middle ground. Part of Dusit Maha Prasat is visible on the right.

Right: Phra Thinang Sivalai Maha Prasat in Sivalai Garden which is situated in the Inner Court.

Below: A ceramic Chinese figure standing outside the entrance to Ho Phra Sulalai.

Opposite: The entrance to Ho Phra That Monthien is decorated in Chinese style. The lacquer doors are adorned with gilded weapons.

and military affairs, who were responsible for national security; here too were the Royal Treasury, the headquarters of the palace guards and other royal offices.

The Central Court was the most important part of the Grand Palace; this was the location of the Phra Maha Prasat and the Phra Maha Monthien Group, which were the centre of government and the royal residence, the place where the King met his officials, performed significant royal ceremonies, and received foreign ambassadors.

The Inner Court, situated behind the Phra Maha Prasat and Phra Maha Monthien Group, was the location of the mansions of the royal consorts, young sons and daughters, and the houses of the king's concubines, as well as officials, guards and attendants, all of whom were female.

The Temple of the Emerald Buddha, situated in the east of the Grand Palace, as well as enshrining the Emerald Buddha, is a compound that contains many buildings of religious importance, many 100s of metres of mural paintings and numerous sculptures.

The Temple of the Emerald Buddha

The temple complex is situated in the north-east corner of the Grand Palace compound. It is surrounded by cloisters on all four sides and these separate it from the royal areas inhabited by the king. Its construction was initiated by King Rama I and as with Wat Mahathat at Sukhothai and Wat Phra Sri Sanphet in Ayutthaya, it is a royal chapel with no resident monks.

Within the complex are many buildings for diverse purposes and in differing styles reflecting the changing architecture of the various reigns. Nevertheless, despite their differences most of the structures adhere strictly to traditional Thai style, their diversity lying rather in certain details or construction materials. The Emerald Buddha Temple dates to the founding of the Grand Palace and Bangkok, but various restorations and additions have been made throughout the nine reigns of the Chakri dynasty. A major restoration has been carried out every fifty years, corresponding with the reigns of King Rama III (r.1824-1851), Rama VII (r.1925-1935) and King Rama IX (r.1946-present).

Above: Two of the pairs of sema *stones surrounding the Ubosot. One of the large giants, the brown Toskiritorn, is visible in the background.*

Opposite: The east side of the Ubosot, or Chapel.

VISITORS' ROUTE

The royal household has determined that visitors enter the complex at the back of the Ubosot (Chapel) through the western gate, and the various buildings along this route are described in this order and numbered accordingly on the plan. Some doubling back is necessary in order not to miss important buildings. Also restoration of certain areas may require changes to the suggested route. Finally, as the visitor proceeds around the complex he or she may wish to look at the Ramakien Murals painted on the **cloister walls** ❶ If you start looking here you will be starting about two thirds of the way through at room 124 out of 178 rooms in total. The starting point of the murals is shown on the plan but this does not fit in with the route.

Once you have left the temple complex you will the visit the residential part of the Grand Palace with the palaces of the former kings and the throne halls which are still used today. The average time for the entire visit depends on the level of interest but if you visit all the sites including the museum you should allow two hours. Shorts and flip flops are not allowed.

Within the Emerald Buddha Temple compound are many diverse buildings. At right is a corner of one of the 12 small pavilions surrounding the Ubosot. Two more are visible in the middle ground. At left is the Phra Sri Rattana Chedi, to its right the Mondop and in the background the prang *atop the roofs of Prasat Phra Thep Bidorn.*

Right: The western facade of the Ubosot, at left, with Ho Rajbongsanusorn in the centre.

Opposite: Plan of the Temple complex.

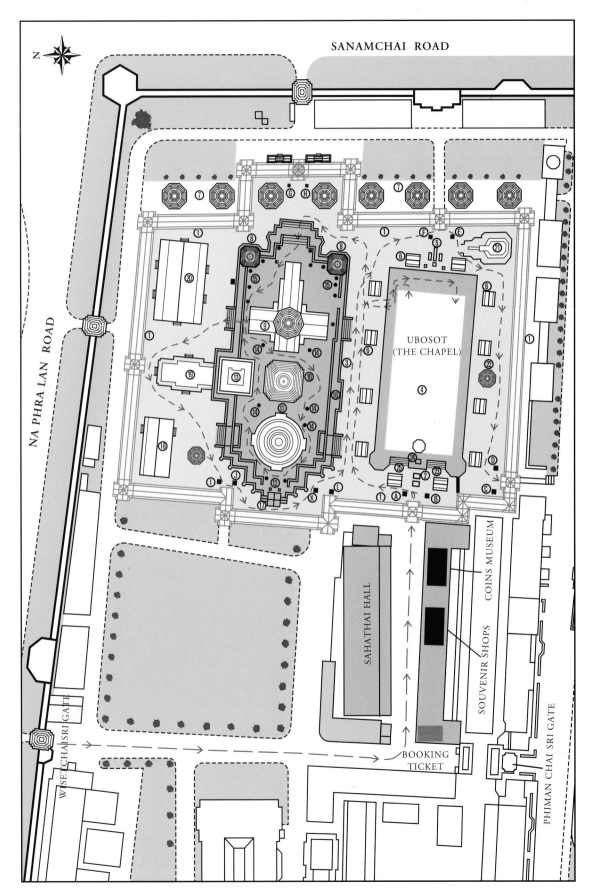

A bronze hermit, or rishi, *is situated at the rear of the Ubosot. Note the gold leaf applied to the base of the statue and the medicinal grinding stones by worshippers.*

Having entered the compound, you will see the first of two large stucco giants. In total, **12 giants**, characters from the **Ramakien** guard the entrances on three sides. A full list is given on pages 40-41. There are two pairs on the eastern side, one pair on the south and three pairs guarding the three entrances on the west. The two guarding this gate are Asakornmarsa, who is purple with a double tier of heads, and Chakrawat, who is white with four heads and eight arms. Both have crowns surmounted by a plume of cockerel feathers. Look to your left and you will see another pair. The white giant Sahasadeja has 1,000 heads arranged in five tiers and 2,000 arms. He stands with Tosakanth who is green.

Immediately in front of you upon entering is the **bronze hermit or rishi ❷**, installed by King Rama III. He was believed to be skilled in traditional medecine and in front of him is a grinding stone where previously practitioners could grind their ingredients and enhance their efficacy.

As you walk across the paved courtyard towards the entrance to the Ubosot (the chapel housing the Emerald Buddha), note the various **Chinese stone carvings ❸**, used as ballast in junks from China during the reign of King Rama III, and the ornamental trees arranged in porcelain planters.

Before entering or after leaving the Ubosot, you should also note the small fenced area containing offerings that have been made to the Emerald Buddha. The figure of the Chinese **Chao Mae Guan Im ❺**, a Bodhisattva in the Mahayana Buddhist tradition, is placed at the foot of a sandstone column topped by a bronze lotus *(see box overleaf)*. She is flanked by two Chinese stone birds – Nok Wayupak. Two lead cows stand facing the gate. These were previously used to stand in front of the royal pavilion during the Royal Ploughing Ceremony in the Fourth Reign. Later during the reign of King Rama V the pavilion was removed and the cattle moved to their present position. The two small Buddhas within this enclosure act as a kind of stand in for the Emerald Buddha. As the lighting of candles and joss sticks is prohibited within the Ubosot, people can make offerings and light candles and joss sticks here instead. Behind this area stand one of the two pairs of giants guarding the eastern side. These two green giants with *naga*-topped crowns are Virunhok and Mangkorngun.

Small Buddha images have been placed outside the Ubosot as substitutes for worshippers wishing to make offerings to the Emerald Buddha, as the lighting of candles and joss sticks is not allowed within the chapel.

Above: People praying in front of the Chao Mae Guan Im enclosure outside the Ubosot.

Left: One of the two lead cows formerly used in the ploughing ceremony.

Right: Close-up of the Chinese goddess, Guan Im.

Below: People thronging in front of the shine lighting joss sticks and offering flowers.

The Legend of Chao Mae Guan Im

Ancient Chinese legends recount the following story about this Goddess of Loving Kindness, known under another name as Avalokitesvara.

She was a Buddhist and the third daughter of a king, who, however, did not respect Buddhism and was enraged with her and her Buddhist practices. He challenged her to prove the power of her Buddhist faith by making a dead bush in the garden which had lost all its leaves, sprout new growth within three days. Using the power of Buddhist meditation she achieved this feat. The king was still not satisfied and told her to change a large iron bar into a small needle. Again she used meditative powers to do as he instructed

The king now ordered her to get married against her wishes and she decided to escape taking with her all the prisoners who her father had tortured and imprisoned. During her flight she had to carry a baby in her arms and look after old people. The king's army followed in hot pursuit to the edge of a river, but the princess used her power to create a bridge and everyone escaped. All those whom she had rescued now venerated her as Chao Mae Guan Im, the Goddess of Loving Kindness who hears the sorrows of the world, and built her a temple.

The king was even angrier and sent a fleet across the river to burn down the temple, but the flames turned back on the troops and burned them, forcing them to flee. The king now fell seriously ill and a treacherous physician seeking to destroy both the king and his daughter said that the only cure was to take the eyes and arms of one his children in order to make the medecine. The king sent some eunuchs to make such a request of Chao Mae Guan Im. She immediately scooped her eyes from their sockets and ordered the eunuch to cut off her arms. Miraculously, the king recovered at once and the princess was reborn with both her eyes and an additional one in the centre of her forehead. Instead of two arms she now had 10, was seated on a lotus floating in the air and was surrounded by an aura. The citizens of that principality all venerated her and finally even her father became a Buddhist convert.

Chao Mae Guan Im is particularly venerated by the Chinese. Indeed, most Chinese households have a small statue or picture of her, believing that she will give blessings and grant requests made to her. She is usually shown as a seated or standing woman, dressed in white, holding either a twig, a rosary or a small bottle of *amritsa* (sacred elixir).

The Ramakien Cloisters ❶

One of the main decorative themes throughout the temple is the *Ramakien*, the Thai version of the Indian epic poem, *The Ramayana*. Thus pairs of giants guard the main gates, monkeys and giants support certain *chedis* and the cloisters contain 178 scenes from the *Ramakien*.

The cloisters form a covered gallery surrounding the entire Emerald Buddha Temple complex. King Rama I commissioned the painting of murals telling the *Ramakien* story based on his own version, which was modified from the *Ramayana*. (The names of the characters are given in their Thai version, with the better-known Indian name in brackets for the principal characters). The relevance of the *Ramayana* story to kings and kingship has long been recognised in Southeast Asia, a prime example being the *Ramayana* reliefs carved by the Khmers at Angkor Wat and many lesser Khmer temples. Phra Ram (Rama), the hero of the epic, is the earthly incarnation of Phra Narai (Vishnu) sent down to help humankind. In Thailand, the king has long been equated with Phra Narai, thus the Ramakien is full of analogies with the king and his beneficent deeds.

Altogether there are 178 panels, with the first panel beginning from the north gate opposite Viharn Yod (19) and then proceeding in an anti-clockwise direction. Below each panel is an abbreviated synopsis of the scene in Thai. In addition there are another 80 mural paintings comprising Phra Narai before his descent to earth as Phra Ram, and various other principal characters from the Ramakien painted on the pillars and corridors leading in from the entrances.

Looking down the cloister. In the foreground is one of the characters from the Ramakien – *Mayarap, one of Tosakanth friends, while the walls behind show narrative scenes.*

The *Ramakien* in Brief *(Numerals in English and Thai refer to the panel numbers of that episode)*

King Rama I wrote his own version of the *Ramakien*, dividing it into five long episodes. The story begins with the rebirth and incarnations of major characters who seem mostly to come from the celestial realm. The hero of the epic, Phra Ram (Rama), is the incarnation of the deity Phra Narai (Vishnu), who was requested to take a human form by the almighty Phra Isuan (Siva) and to vanquish the evil power perpetrated by demons possessed of magical powers. Phra Ram's lineage on earth is given as well as the the founding of the magnificent state of Ayutthaya (Ayodhya) with King Tosarot (Dasaratha), Phra Ram's earthly father, as its ruler. (The early part of the story is not illustrated in the main murals but on the side panels and is difficult to track).

Phra Isuan's loyal gate keeper, Nontuk received magical powers from the deities and, not unlike many who received similar awards, abused it by ruthlessly slaying deities and humans. Nontuk's gift from Phra Isuan was a jeweled finger that can point death to anyone he wishes. Realizing these evil doings, Phra Narai, at the request of Phra Isuan, tricks Nontuk into pointing a finger at himself causing his own death. Before dying, he pledges vengeance on Phra Narai.

Reborn on earth, Nontuk takes the form of the 10-faced and 20-armed Tosakanth (Ravana), the demon king of the Longka city state. The story then turns to the origin of the monkey race, ruled by the incarnate of deities like Pali, son of Phra Indra (Indra), Sukreep, son of Phra Athit (the sun god), and Hanuman, son of Phra Pai (the wind god), who later becomes Phra Ram's chief soldier. Monto, formerly a deity who later becomes Tosakanth's consort, is born on earth around the same time.

Meanwhile, in the magnificent city state of Ayutthaya, the benevolent King Tosarot rules beside his three consorts, none of whom have given him any children. Concerned about his succession, the court hermit offers to perform a special ritual involving divine power for the begetting of sons. Thus occur the royal births of Phra Ram, Phra Prot (Bharat), Phra Lak (Lakshman) and Phra Satarud (Shatrughan). Phra Ram is the incarnate of Phra Narai, Phra Lak is the incarnate of the god's serpent throne (Sesha) and conch shell; Phra Prot is the incarnate of his discus, and Phra Satarud the incarnate of his sceptre.

In Lonka, Tosakanth's consort, Monto, gives birth to Sida (Sita), the incarnate of Phra Narai's consort. Pipek, Tosakanth's brother, who happens to be an astrologer, predicts that Sida will destroy the demon race so Tosakanth places her in a ceramic jar and sets it adrift along a waterway. The infant Sida is later found by King Chanok of the Mithila principality who was at a hermitage nearby **(room 1/๑)**.

At the palace in Mithila, Sida grows up to be a beautiful young princess and King Chanok plans to find a man worthy of her. He announces to city states and principalities far and wide that whosoever can lift the divine bow of Phra Isuan will marry his daughter. The princes of Ayutthaya hear this news while journeying through a forest. Phra Ram shows great prowess in lifting the bow to the astonishment and delight of all and is thus awarded the hand of the most beautiful and sought after princess **(room 4-5/๔ - ๕)**. King Chanok sends an emissary to invite rulers and their consorts to attend the royal wedding. The spectacular matrimonial ritual of Phra Ram's marriage to Sida is remniscent of the traditional Thai nuptial ceremony which combines Brahmanic rituals with Buddhist prayers **(room 8/๘)**.

Phra Ram.

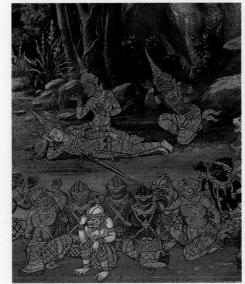

Phra Lak.

Now in the city of Keetkin where the monkey king Pali rules, Sukreep, his half brother, is suspected of being treacherous and is banished. Consequently Sukreep joins Phra Ram's army. In the meantime, at Ayutthya, King Tosarot decides to hold a coronation ceremony for Phra Ram, his eldest and favorite son. A hunchback maid of one of Phra Ram's stepmothers, Kaiyaket, who was ridiculed by the young Phra Ram many years earlier, requests Kaiyaket to remind King Tosarot to grant her one wish which he pledged to her many years ago, when Kaiyaket had helped him keep the wheel of his chariot from falling apart. Her wish is that the king banish Phra Ram into the forest for 14 years thus paving the way for Phra Prot, her own son, to be crowned instead. Distraught, King Tosarot, nevertheless, keeps his word and complies with her demand. After an audience with the king, Phra Ram willingly leaves for the forest with Phra Lak and Sida **(room 16/๑๖)**. King Tosarot never recovers from parting with his beloved son and soon passes away **(room 17/๑๗)**. Saddened by the king's death, Phra Prot, Phra Satarud, and the late king's consorts implore Phra Ram to return and rule Ayutthaya **(room 18/๑๘)**. But Phra Ram insists that he fulfill his father's wish in staying away for 14 years.

In Longka, Tosakanth decides to go travelling with his queen, Monto, leaving the kingdom under the care of Chiw-ha, his sister's husband. After a week's vigil, Chiw-ha decides to sleep, but he takes preventive measures by transforming into a huge demon and using his tongue to shield Longka. When Tosakanth returns, he cannot find his city and thinks that it has been destroyed by the enemy. In despair, he throws his discus onto the site where Longka once stood. The discus accidentally cuts Chiw-ha's tongue, immediately killing him **(room 21/๒๑)**. Samanakka, Tosakanth's sister, and bereaved wife of Chiw-ha, enters the forest to calm herself. She comes near the forest abode of Phra Ram, Phra Lak and Sida. Catching sight of Phra Ram bathing in a pool, she falls in love with him and transforms herself into a beautiful woman but her attempts to seduce him are in vain. Infuriated, Samanakka tries to harm Sida but fortunately Phra Lak comes in time and slices off the mouth, ear, nose and feet of the demoness **(room 22/๒๒)**.

The wounded Samanakka journeys to request three of her brothers to take revenge on Phra Ram. To her dismay, she finds that he has already killed them **(room 23/๒๓)**. Now Samanakka becomes even more vengeful. She describes the exquisite beauty of Sida to Tosakanth, persuading him to abduct the fair maiden and make her his consort in Longka. The demon king, unaware that Sida is his own daughter, requests the hermit Mareet to transform himself into a golden deer in order to lure Phra Ram and Phra Lak away and clear the way for Sida's abduction.

The trick works and the hermit princes follow the golden deer while Tosakanth carries Sida off into the sky towards Longka. Spotting them, the kind bird Sdayu unsuccessfully tries to rescue her from the demon. Tosakanth takes off Sida's magic ring from her finger and throws it at Sdayu **(room 24/๒๔)**, who catches it with its beak and takes it to Phra Ram, telling him about Sida's abduction before it dies **(room 25/๒๕)**. And now the long search for Sida begins. Phra Ram is offered help by Hanuman, the white monkey who cannot die because the wind god will always revive him **(room 26/๒๖)**.

Meanwhile, in Longka, Tosakanth takes Sida to his garden to woo her but she tries to kill herself. Hanuman arrives in time to help her by presenting to Sida her ring and *sabai* or decorative cloth **(room 34/๓๔)**. Indrachit, Tosakanth's son, catches Hanuman and punishes him cruelly. Indrachit has the power to transform into the god Indra, a skill which he learned from the hermit Kobut. Hanuman cunningly devises a means to burn Longka and escape. He asks Tosakanth to set him on fire and then runs into every building until the whole city is aflame. Of course the wind revives Hanuman back to life again **(room 36/๓๖)**.

In Longka, Tosakanth banishes his brother, the demon Pipek, who prophesied that Tosakanth will eventually be killed by Phra Ram **(room 40/๔๐)**. Pipek joins Phra Ram's army **(room 41/๔๑)**. Later Tosakanth asks the demoness Benyakai to transform herself into a lifeless Sida. He then carries the transformed Benyakai to the river where she floats down towards Phra Ram. The demon king thinks that Phra Ram, fooled into thinking that Sida has died, will retreat **(room 45/๔๕)**.

In the meantime, Hanuman's soldiers build a causeway to Longka **(room 46/๔๖)**. In the battle between Indrachit and Phra Lak, the former offers Tosakanth a ritual to enhance his arrows. During the ritual, Chompuwarat, one of Phra Ram's chief soldiers, transforms himself into a bear and destroys the tree under which Indrachit is seated **(room 72/๗๒)**. Tosakanth asks his demon allies, Moon-plum and the latter's elder brother, Sahasadeja to join the fight against Phra Ram **(room 83/๘๓)**. During the battle, Phra Lak kills Moon-plum while Hanuman tricks the demons by transforming himself into an ordinary white monkey and kills Sahasadeja with a magic club **(room 84/๘๔)**.

In a subsequent battle, Sattasoon makes himself invisible so that he can kill the monkey soldiers. Sattasoon's newphew, Virunchambang, cannot fight Phra Ram and flees to hide in the ocean foam **(room 92/๙๒)**. Hanuman follows, kills him and brings the demon's head to Phra Ram. After many battles have been fought and won by Phra Ram's army with Hanuman as the commander, Phra Ram engages in a single combat with Tosakanth. At long last he succeeds in killing the demon of demons **(room 109/๑๐๙)**.

At the end of Phra Ram's 14-year exile, the forest dwellers plead that he return to rule over Ayutthaya **(room 120/๑๒๐)**. At once Phra Ram tells Hanuman to inform his father's consorts and his brothers of his intended home coming. At long last, Phra Ram ascends the throne of

Sida.

Tosakanth.

Ayutthaya which had become greater than ever before with newly-conquered territory. Phra Prot and Phra Satarud are sent to rule the states of Kaiyaket; the monkey warrior Sukreep is sent to rule over Keetkin and Phra Lak stays by his beloved brother's side, to help rule Ayutthaya **(room 121/๑๒๑)**. Phra Ram then commissions the founding of Nopburi city and makes Hanuman its ruler **(room 122/๑๒๒)**.

After Tosakanth's death, Pipek ascends the Longka throne but troubles begin to brew when Longka is besieged by King Chakrawat, Tosakanth's friend and ruler of the Maliwan state **(room 129/๑๒๙)**.

Phra Prot and Phra Satarud are sent to help Pipek **(room 131/๑๓๑)**. Thereafter ensues the battles at Maliwan where Hanuman helps Phra Prot destroy the two defences of fire and venemous sea water protecting the town **(room 138/๑๓๘)**. Chakrawat now sends his son Ban-laijak into combat but Phra Prot manages to kill him **(room 143/๑๔๓)**. In the last battle scene, Phra Prot aims his arrow at Chakrawat, killing him instantly. As Chakrawat falls, he sees that both princes are incarnates of the god Narai's weapons and in his last breath, he asks them to pardon him **(room 153/๑๕๓)**.

In a memorable episode, Phra Ram and Sida are relaxing in the forest. While she bathes in the pond, the demoness Adun, Tosakanth's cousin, envies her beauty and transforms herself into a maid **(room 157/๑๕๗)**. Adun tricks Sida into drawing the portrait of Tosakanth. Once the picture is drawn, the demoness possesses it and no matter what is done, the portrait cannot be erased. When Phra Ram finds the portrait, he is fooled into thinking that Sida was unfaithful to him during her abduction by Tosakanth. In anger, he orders Phra Lak to take her deep into the forest, kill her, slit her chest and bring her heart back to him. As Phra Lak is about to cut Sida's throat, a garland appears around her neck to protect her. Seeing this, he lets her go. On the way back, he finds a dead deer which the god Indra left on the path. He cuts it open and takes its heart to Phra Ram **(room 158/๑๕๘)**. Indra then transforms himself into a buffalo and leads Sida to a hermitage. Here the hermit Watchamareuk builds a cottage for her and she later gives birth to Phra Ram's son, naming him Phra Mongkut. Another boy, Phra Lop is magically created by the hermit and becomes Phra Mongkut's playmate and adopted brother **(room 159/๑๕๙)**.

One day, while testing their bows and arrows in the forest, Phra Mongkut topples an immense sacred tree with his magic arrow **(room 160/๑๖๐)**. On hearing the mighty tree fall, Phra Ram appeases the gods by performing the ritual of releasing his own horse. In this ancient Indian rite, a white steed belonging to royalty is elaborately decorated and released so that it can visit states and principalities. The people of the places visited must welcome it with pomp and pageantry. Any town which does not welcome the steed is punished by the army that accompanies it **(room 161/๑๖๑)**.

Upon seeing the horse, Phra Mongkut tries to mount him. Hanuman tries to stop him but is caught and tied up by Phra Mongkut and Phra Lop. Sida gives Phra Lop her magic ring and with the help of a celestial being, goes to the aid of her son who manages to escape to the forest **(room 163/๑๖๓)**. Phra Ram, who at this time is not aware that Phra Mongkut is his own son, goes after the two boys and forces them to fight against each other. Since their celestial weapons cannot harm one another, Phra Ram realizes that Phra Mongkut is his own son **(room 164/๑๖๔)**.

To prove that she did not betray Phra Ram, Sida decides to walks on fire. As she steps onto the burning flames, a lotus rises to hold and protect her. Assured that Sida never betrayed him **(room 111/๑๑๑)**, Phra Ram thinks of a way to lure her back to Ayutthaya. He pretends to be dead and then orders Hanuman to inform Sida. When Sida comes to pay homage to his body, Phra Ram opens his eyes to see her in her grief. Realizing that she has been tricked, she prays to mother earth to make way for her to descend into the underworld of the Naga king **(room 165/๑๖๕)**.

Indrajit

Sahasadeja.

When Pipek sees the grief-stricken Phra Ram, he advises him to roam the forests in penitance for one year. Phra Rama agrees and is accompanied by Phra Lak, Hanuman, and a monkey army led by Sukreep **(room 166/๑๖๖)**. In the forest the royal brothers and their entourage encounter many battles with demons and are always victorious. On their return to Ayutthaya, Phra Isuan helps to reunite Phra Ram and Sida by inviting both to meet him at Mount Sumeru at the center of the universe. Here they reconcile their love for each other and return hand in hand to Ayutthaya **(room 171/๑๗๑)**.

In the last episode, the demon Kontam captures the town of Kaiyaket belonging to Phra Prot's maternal grandfather. Phra Ram sends Phra Prot, Phra Satarud, Phra Mongkut and Phra Lop to recapture the town **(room 178/๑๗๘)**.

A eulogy for King Rama I is given at the end of this version of the *Ramakien*, dated 1797.

Hanuman.

Pali.

Sukreep.

Detail of Asakornmarsa's face.

Detail of Sahasadeja's face.

*Opposite: The architecture shown in the
murals is very similar to the actual
architecture of the Grand Palace.*

Above: Room 53 shows Hanuman swallowing Phra Ram's pavilion while Mayarap plays the flute to lull the monkey troops to sleep.

Opposite above: Nang Supanmacha, Tosakanth's daughter from his union with a fish, tries to destroy the road which is being built by the monkey troops. Room 47.

Below: Room 113 shows the scene when Tosakanth's younger brother supervises his older brother's funeral.

A

The Twelve Giants (A-L)

Around the cloisters pairs of giants guard the entrances on three sides:
The two eastern entrances, The first door in line with the Prasat Thep Bidorn has **Indrajit (A)** in green with a bamboo shoot on his crown and **Suryapop (B)** who is red with a similar crown. The second eastern door aligns with the Ubosot and is guarded by a green and a purple giant whose crowns are topped with *nagas:* **Virunhok (C)** and **Mangkorngun (D)**.

The southern door, Srirattana Sasada, is guarded by two giants with elephant trunks instead of noses – **Totkiritorn (E)** who is red and **Totkirijun (F)** who is dark green. Both their crowns are topped with bamboo shoots.

The western side has three doors. The first (where you enter the temple compound) aligns with the rear of the Ubosot and is guarded by two giants whose crowns are topped by cockerel's tails. The white giant, **Chakrawat (G)** with four heads and eight arms is paired by **Asakornmarsa (H)** who is dark purple and has a double tier of heads. The second door aligns with the western side of Phra Sri Rattana Chedi. The white giant **Sahasadeja (I)** has one thousand heads arranged in five tiers and two thousand arms. He stands with **Tosakanth (J)** who is green. He has three tiers of three heads and one on top. His crown is topped with a *chai*. The third door aligns with the northern side of Phra Sri Rattana Chedi and is once again guarded by giants with cockerel tail crowns – the navy coloured **Viruncham-bang (K)** and his companion the pale mauve **Mayarap (L)**.

E

I

B

C

D

F

G

H

J

K

L

The Ubosot *(Chapel)* ❹

The Ubosot is located in the southern sector of the temple compound and is the principal building, being larger than all surrounding structures. To enter the Ubosot, the visitor must pass through two walls. These separate the building from the rest of the compound, thereby emphasising its sacred nature. The wall is topped by double *sema* stones covered with gold leaf. Such stones traditionally designate a Buddhist building where the ordination of monks may be carried out.

Detail of one of the pediments showing Phra Narai on garuda.

Above: A high level view of the Ubosot from the west.

The chapel was built during the reign of King Rama I in 1783 in order to house the Emerald Buddha statue which the King had taken from Vientiane in 1778. Previously it had been housed in the nearby Emerald Buddha hall on the Thonburi side of the river. Today this hall has been transformed into the chapel of Wat Arun on the opposite bank of the river. The Emerald Buddha was installed ceremonially on 22 June 1784.

Before examining the Ubosot itself, the visitor should note the **open pavilions** ❻, of which there are twelve, surrounding the Ubosot. With grey marble bases, they were constructed for the faithful to sit and listen to sermons. They were built during the reign of King Rama I.

Exterior

The visitor should make sure to look at the chapel from top to bottom as every part is a prime example of the finest workmanship of the early Rattanakosin period. In addition, many parts of the architecture are full of symbolism.

The carved wooden pediments covered with gold leaf bear representations of Phra Narai (Vishnu) on his mount *garuda* (half bird-half man), the latter holding the tail of a *naga* (mythical serpent) in either hand, against a background of foliate *kanok* motifs and angels. In Brahmin belief Vishnu on Garuda symbolizes the king, thus any chapel bearing this motif on the pediment is one constructed by the king. The *kanok* motif derives from the Ayutthaya period. The pediment is edged with carved decoration terminating in *hang hong,* which are *naga* heads, while at its apex on the roof ridge are the two gilded *chofa* representing the head of *garuda.* The jagged edge running up the edge of the roofs known as the *lamyong* represent the *garuda's* arms.*(see* Architectural Elements *on page 152-153).*

The lower edge of the roof is decorated with bells with *bhodi* leaf shaped ringers. When the wind blows their musical tinkling is meant to make the visitor feel that he or she has entered a sacred realm.

Eave brackets rising from the columns are known as *kuantuay* and are in the shape of *nagas* with heads pointing down, signifying the *naga* as protector of the Buddha before he attained enlightenment.

The square columns have 12-redented corners covered in gold leaf, while the main body of the pillars is covered with glass mosaic in geometric patterns. The capitals are in the form of

Detail of the lower portion of the roof structure, showing the bells with bhodi *leaf ringers and the* kuantuay. *Note also the small carved dragon in the background.*

Below left and middle: Details of the roof showing the hang hong, *the* lamyong *and bells.*

Below right: Details of the redenting on the columns and the glass mosaic.

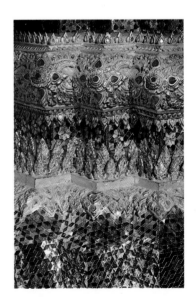

Detail of the Chinese porcelain.

Detail of grey marble.

Detail of frieze around the base of the Ubosot wall.

Above: Bronze, gilded garudas *wearing crowns and* raiment *surround the base of the Ubosot.*

lotus petals also covered with glass mosaic. There are 48 outer columns in all. Between the columns is a low wall whose exterior face is decorated with Chinese porcelain with a flower pattern ordered during the reign of King Rama III. The interior face is grey marble carved with flower arrangements in low relief, also from China.

The exterior walls of the Ubosot itself are covered with porcelain tiles decorated with gold mosaic in foliate *kanok* motifs designed in the reign of King Rama III. The base of the wall is extremely ornate being surrounded by 112 richly-ornamented gold-leaf *garudas* standing on *nagas* and grasping their tales. Below is more foliage decoration.

The doors are surmounted by carvings in what is termed *mondop* style i.e. carvings echoing the tiered roofs as found atop royal palaces. There are six doors in all, three on the eastern side and three on the west. On both sides, the central door, which is slightly larger than those on either side, is used only by the king. The exterior of the doors are mother-of-pearl inlay in the form of foliage terminating in various mythical animals believed to inhabit the Himavamsa Forest. Their workmanship is extremely fine and sought to rival that of the Ayutthaya period. Examples of doors which are from Ayutthaya may be seen at the Viharn Yod (No. 19), while another pair are at Wat Phra Sri Rattana Mahathat, Phitsanulok. The interior panels of the doors are gold lacquer with lotus bud designs.

The walls of the Ubosot are very thick and on the extremely wide inner doorframes of each door are Chinese Guardians with pikes in stucco covered with gold leaf and glass mosaic. They were created by King Rama III and gilded by King Rama IV. Similarly, within the window frames may be seen gilded stucco *devas,* or deities, holding swords.

Above: Six bronze Khmer lion guardians stand in pairs at the base of each set of steps. The middle pair are the originals from which the others were copied. The top of the doors are in mondop style. Note also the gold mosaic in kanok motif of the exterior walls.

The window surrounds are similar to those above the doors. The exterior window panels are in mother-of-pearl, with gold on red lacquer on the interior.

12 bronze lion guardians stand at the base of the steps leading into the Ubosot. In style they copy the style of stone lions from the Bayon period of the Khmer empire which stand on either side of the steps ascending to the Royal Pantheon. Originally they were believed to be Khmer bronzes but Professor Jean Boisselier determined that they were Thai copies rather than Khmer originals. Others continue to believe that the two guarding the central door on the eastern side were brought from Cambodia on the orders of King Rama I and that the other 10 were copied from these.

Left, below and opposite below left: The mother-of-pearl inlaid doors show mythical animals from the Himavamsa Forest. They date from the First Reign.

Above right: The inner part of the window embrasures are decorated with stucco, gilded devas.

Above left and below right: The walls of the Ubosot are over 1 metre thick and the inner parts of the door frames are decorated with stucco and gilded Chinese guardians.

Interior

The interior of the Ubosot is richly decorated. The wooden ceiling is painted in red and gold and decorated with silver glass mosaic in star formation to simulate heaven. All four walls are painted with murals relating to the Buddha. Then, apart from the Emerald Buddha itself, the visitor will be impressed by the large number of other Buddha images surrounding the ornately carved central altar, described on page 52.

Above: The interior of the Ubosot showing the Emerald Buddha in his winter raiment and the accompanying Buddha images. Behind the mural painting shows the Traibhum, or Buddhist cosmology.

Opposite: The rear of the Ubosot with Phra Sri Rattana Chedi visible in the background. At left, part of the Phra Photithat Phiman.

Detail of the lower part of the altar.

The Emerald Buddha

The Emerald Buddha is in fact not emerald but carved from a solid piece of jade, measuring 66 cm high including the base and 48.3 cm wide at the widest point. The image is seated in the meditation posture with the right leg folded over the left. According to Prince Subhadradis Diskul such iconography is consistent with the late Northern Thai, or late Chieng Saen style, but he has also speculated that the style is reminiscent of some Buddha images from Southern India or Sri Lanka, where the meditation posture was more popular than in Thailand.

The image was brought to Bangkok from Vientiane by King Rama I, but before that time the image had already travelled extensively *(see map)*. A chronicle relates that in 1434 AD lightning struck a chedi in Chieng Rai revealing a stucco-covered Buddha image. When this stucco began to flake off the Emerald Buddha, so-called on account of its green colour was revealed. Hearing of the find, King Samfangkaen, King of Chieng Mai which had suzerainty over Chieng Rai, ordered that the image be brought to the capital. However the elephant bearing the Emerald Buddha repeatedly turned off towards Lampang and thus the king allowed the statue to remain in Lampang. Later in 1468 in the reign of King Tilokaraj of Chieng Mai it was finally brought to Chieng Mai. In 1551 the then king of Chieng Mai died without a son and as his daughter was married to a Lao prince the image was taken to Luang Prabang by the prince who was now King Chaichettha of Laos. In 1564 King Chaichettha fled the Burmese down to Vientiane taking the Emerald Buddha with him. The image was to remain there for 214 years until in 1778, Phraya Chakri, as a general in the army of King Taksin, captured Vientiane and brought the Emerald Buddha back to Thailand. It was first installed in Thonburi in pavilion next to the Ubosot of Wat Arun, and was moved to the temple of the Emerald Buddha on 22 March 1784. At that time two sets of robes, one for the hot season and one for the rainy season, were provided. Later, during the reign of King Rama III, a further set for the winter season was added. In 1997, the Royal Treasury Department was granted permission by His Majesty the King to create three new sets, with the old set being viewable in the museum.

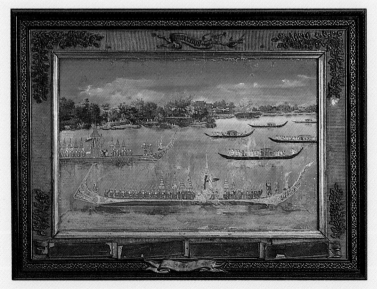

The procession taking the Emerald Buddha to Thonburi. Painted during the reign of King Rama V.

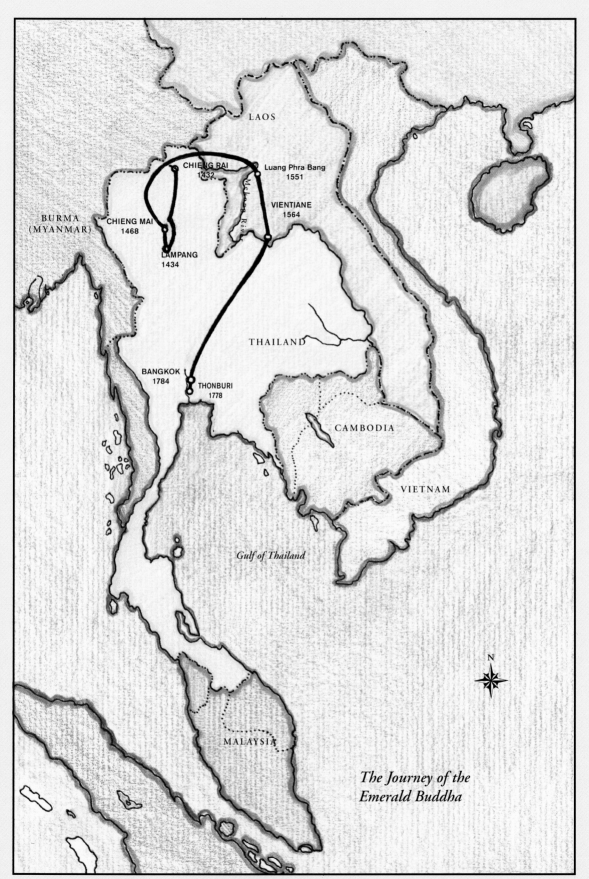

The Journey of the
Emerald Buddha

Opposite: In the foreground is the large statue of Phra Buddha Yodfa, while on the far left is its twin, Phra Buddha Lertla. Behind, the mural painting depicts the life of the Buddha.

Below: Diagram showing the principal Buddha images within the Ubosot. The key to Nos. D-O may be found overleaf.

The **Emerald Buddha** Ⓐ is placed on an intricately carved and gilded wooden throne, known as a *busabok*, which dates from the First Reign. As with others of similar type, it is in the form of a miniature *prasat* with a five-tiered roof, but the workmanship is of exceptionally high quality. The base on which it stands was heightened during the reign of King Rama III by incorporating the funeral bier used during the funeral of King Rama II.

A pair of **Large Crowned Standing Bronze Buddhas** flank the main throne. In the Pacifying the Ocean Attitude, they stand approximately 3 m high, are encased in gold and precious stones, and weigh 70 kgs. They were cast on the orders of King Rama III in 1841 and dedicated to the memory of King Rama I, his grandfather (to the north, on the right) and King Rama II, his father (to the south, on the left). The statue dedicated to King Rama I was named Phra Buddha Yodfa Chulalok Ⓑ, while the other was called Phra Buddha Lertla Supalai Ⓒ A proclamation confirmed that this was the name by which these deceased kings should henceforth be called instead of the popular appellations of Beginning Reign and Middle Reign, with its unpropitious implication that King Rama III's reign would be the last. Later, King Rama IV placed a relic of the Buddha within the crowns of both images.

Above: Phra Sambuddha Panni. The style of the robes which mimic real fabric and the lack of the protuberance emanating from the Buddha's head is typical of the Fourth Reign.

Top left: Detail from one of two large Standing Buddhas.

Top Right: The heavily ornamented torso and hands of one of the Standing Buddhas.

These two Buddha images were worshipped during the ceremony in which officials drank the consecrated water thereby swearing their allegiance to the king.

10 Crowned Standing Buddhas ●-● in the Pacifying the Ocean attitude. These bronze images encased in gold are arranged in pairs in three tiers with only one pair on the lowest level and four on the upper two. They were created by successive kings of the Chakri Dynasty in order to commemorate specific members of the royal family. Those whose robes flare out at the bottom represent male members of the royal family, while those whose robes fall straight represent women. On the lower tier that at north commemorates Princess Absorn Sudathep ●, the daughter of King Rama III, while opposite stands of Queen Srisulalai ●, the mother of King Rama III. On the middle tier: front south is the image dedicated to the Deputy King of King Rama II ●, front north is for King Rama II ●, back south commemorates Princess Srisunthornthep ●, daughter of King Rama I, while back north is dedicated to the Second Deputy King from the reign of King Rama I ●. Those on the upper tier are dedicated as follows: front south is in honour of the Deputy King of King Rama I ●, front north to King Rama I ●, at the back to the two elder sisters of King Rama I, on the south to Princess Srisudarat ●, on the north to Princess Thepsudawadi ●. The Buddha known as **Phra Sambuddha Panni ●**, is situated on the lowest tier of the base of the Emerald Buddha. Prince Mongkut, as he then was, commissioned its casting when he was the abbot of Wat Bovornives in order to house his astrological chart and a Buddha

relic. Once he ascended the throne as King Mongkut, Rama IV, he swopped this image with the Phra Buddha Sihing which once occupied this position in the Third Reign, placing the latter back to the National Museum. The form of the Buddha is a break with traditional iconography in that there is no cranial protuberance and the robe is very naturalistic and highly pleated.

A very small silver Buddha now blackened by time is called **Phra Chai Lang Chang** ◉. The image is in the Meditation Posture and holds a fan in front of his face. It was extremely important to King Rama I, who took it with him into battle on the back of his elephant.

In front of the main altar is a marble throne brought back by King Rama V from his second trip to Europe in 1908.

Above: Details show the Emerald Buddha in the three different sets of robes for the appropriate season. These are the original sets which are now on display in the museum.

Top left: Rainy season attire.

Top right: Winter raiment.

Middle right: Summer robes.

Right: Phra Chai Lang Chang.

His Majesty the King presiding over a royal ceremony within the Ubosot.

People praying and making obeisance to the Emerald Buddha.

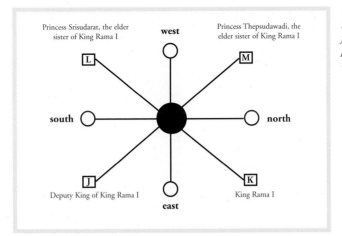

Upper Tier

The location of the Buddha images commemorating former Kings, Queens and princesses of the first three reigns.

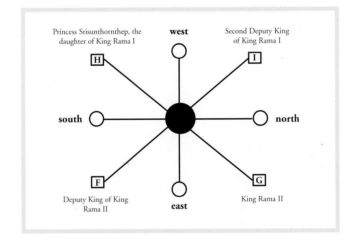

Middle Tier

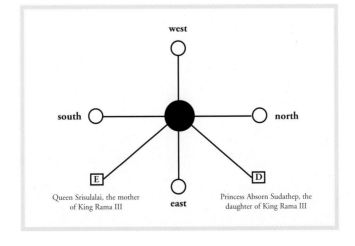

Lower Tier

Mural Paintings

Eastern Wall
The upper level represents the Buddha subduing Mara and his attainment of Enlightenment. Painted in the reign of King Rama I.

Over the central door, Phra Dharani, the Earth Goddess, is seen squeezing her hair. The association of the Earth Goddess with the Buddha relates to the episode when Mara asked the Buddha why he was entitled to attain enlightenment and to which he replied he had attained sufficient merit in his past lives. In confirmation, the Earth Goddess wrung out of her hair the water representing all the Buddha's deeds of merit, thereby drowning Mara's army. Even today when a person makes merit, afterwards water is poured onto the ground so that the Earth Goddess may bear witness and the merit may pass to dead loved ones.

Western Wall
The entire wall is given over to the Traibhum, the Buddhist cosmology comprising the Three Worlds of Desire, Form and Non-Form.

Northern and Southern Walls
Above the windows there would formerly have been painted the assembly of the *devas*, or celestial beings, as was customary during the late Ayutthaya period. However, during the restoration under King Rama III, these figures were overpainted with scenes from the Life of the Buddha.

Above: Detail from the mural painting on the eastern wall, upper level, showing a detail from the battle between Mara's army and the devas.

Left: Detail showing a scene from the life of the Buddha.

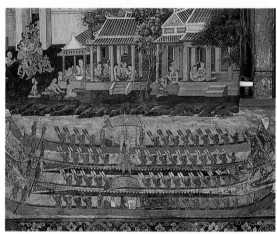

Above the windows glass triptychs show scenes from the Life of the Buddha.

Top left and top right: Between the windows are scenes from the Jataka Tales.
Right: Shows a typical Thai house on stilts.

Left: The annual Ploughing Ceremony.

Middle left: Northern wall, lower level: Procession on land.

Middle right: Southern wall, lower level: a water-borne procession.

Opposite: The marriage ceremony of Prince Siddharta.

Between the windows are painted scenes from the Jataka Tales, or previous lives of the Buddha.

On the northern wall below the windows is shown a royal procession by land, while the southern wall below the windows shows a royal procession by water.

Apart from the Buddha images and mural paintings described above, the Ubosot is decorated with many items installed by various kings over the past 200 plus years. Examples include the triptychs on glass of the Life of the Buddha above every window and door; or the lacquer and gold screen; or the marble pulpit and marble vases.

Upon exiting the Ubosot retrace your steps somewhat to climb the steps to the upper terrace on the eastern side. On the way you can notice two of the eight prangs which were constructed by King Rama I to the east of the Ubosot.

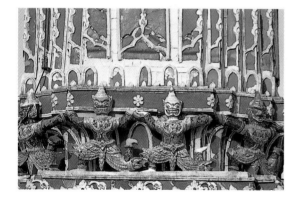

Above: Giants surround the neck of the prang.

Top: Four of the eight prangs *which run along the eastern side of the Emerald Buddha temple.*

Right: Niche on the reddish brown prang *which is dedicated to the Bodhisattvas.*

Row of Eight Prangs ➐

These were covered with porcelain in the reign of King Rama III. Then in the reign of King Rama IV in order to accomodate the Royal Pantheon part of the eastern wall was extended and two of the *prangs* were enclosed within the temple compound. These *prangs* were dedicated to various aspects of Buddhism. From north to South: white – the Buddha, mid-blue – the Dhamma (the scriptures), pink – the Sangha (the Buddhist monks), green – the Bikshuni (the Buddhist nuns), dark purple – Pacchekabodhi Buddhas (those who attained Englightenment but did not preach), pale blue – the Chakravarti (previous emperors of the kingdom), reddish brown – the Bodhisattva (the Buddha in his previous lives), and yellow – the Maitreya (the future Buddha). The style of these *prangs* is typically Rattanakosin, being smaller, thinner and taller than those of Ayutthaya. A frieze of stucco demons surrounds the neck of the *prang* and from their Chinese style King Chulalongkorn believed that these dated from the Third Reign.

Above: One of the two golden chedis.

Above left: Giants and monkeys, characters from the Ramakien *epic, support the* chedis *around their bases.*

Several important buildings are grouped together on a raised terrace. They are interspersed with smaller monuments and various decorative figures. You should also notice the *Phanom Mak,* which are stucco models of the offerings traditionally placed in front of Buddha images. Measuring approximately 2.5 metres high there are eight in all placed at intervals around the terrace. Constructed during the reign of King Rama VI, they are painted green to mimic the originals which are made from banana leaves.

Two Golden Chedis ❽

This pair of chedis are situated to the east of the Royal Pantheon. They were built by King Rama I for his father (on the south) and mother (on the north). The square, tiered base has redented corners and the body is decorated. They are covered with copper and then gold leaf. The unusual feature of these chedis are the monkeys and giants from the *Ramakien* supporting the structure. Altogether there are four monkeys and 16 giants around each, with the colour and clothing of each monkey or giant identifying it with a particular character in the *Ramakien.*

Prasat Phra Thep Bidorn *(Royal Pantheon)* ❾

This building is the most important on the upper terrace and aligns with the entrance gate surmounted by a Thai-style stucco and porcelain crown. The two giants guarding this entrance are Indrajit in green with a bamboo shoot finial to his crown and Suryapop who is red with a similar crown. Behind may be seen the top of the Sawadee Sopha Gate (which is only opened on Buddhist holy days).

Prasat Phra Thep Bidorn was constructed by King Rama IV with the intention of housing the Emerald Buddha as he considered that the Ubosot was too low. However once the building was completed it was too small for royal ceremonies and, accordingly, other relics were installed instead. Later towards the end of the Fifth Reign a fire entirely destroyed the superstructure of the building necessitating its repair. Subsequently it housed statues of the five Chakri kings from the First to the Fifth Reigns. It acquired the name of Prasat Phra Thep Bidorn, translated in English as Royal Pantheon, during the reign of King Rama VI (1910-1925).

The balustrades of the grey marble steps terminate in gilded five-headed nagas.

Top: The eastern facade of Prasat Phra Thep Bidorn, flanked by the Two Golden Chedis.

Left: The north porch of Prasat Phra Thep Bidorn with one of the Phanom Mak in the foreground.

Architecturally this cruciform building is second only to the Ubosot in importance and was constructed with great finesse. In the middle, where the four arms of the cross meet, rises a stucco *prang* decorated with porcelain, in contrast with the *mondop*-style spires which ornament the buildings used as royal residences.

Of particular note are the pediments in which King Rama IV broke with the tradition of showing Phra Narai on *garuda* in order to represent the various reigns of the Chakri dynasty. Thus the northern pediment has a symbol shaped like the Thai numeral one, which represents the reign of King Rama I, the southern pediment shows *garuda* and *naga* representing King Rama II, the western pediment shows a tri-partite pavilion representing King Rama III, while the eastern pediment shows the crown *(mongkut)* symbolising the reign of King Rama IV whose name was King Mongkut. As with the Ubosot, small bells hang from the lower edge of the roof creating a soothing tinkling if there is a light breeze.

The walls of the pantheon are decorated with pale blue porcelain tiles with floral motifs which were ordered by King Rama III to decorate Wat Arun, but arrived too late for that temple and were therefore used here.

The door and window surrounds are in the form of Thai-style crowns decorated with gold leaf and glass mosaic. Formerly the door and window panels were mother-of-pearl inlay portraying five royal Thai decorations – Nopparat, Chakri, Chulachomklao, White Elephant and Crown of Siam. However, today they are gold lacquer with a design of lotus buds and angels. The panels to either side of the doors and the windows still have stucco and gilded emblems from the First to the Fifth Reigns.

When the restoration of the Emerald Buddha complex was carried out during the Fifth Reign, the steps were refashioned in marble with railings terminating in a five-headed crowned and gilded *naga* known as Naga Jum Laeng.

The square pillars are decorated with gold and mirror mosaic on the redented corners while the main body of the pillars are covered with Chinese porcelain arranged in geometric design.

Currently Prasat Phra Thep Bidorn is only opened on Chakri Day, 6 April, and on the Coronation Anniversary on 5 May, in order that the King and the populace may pay hommage.

Above: The eastern pediment with the emblem of King Rama IV, which is a Thai crown.

Top: The southern pediment bears a garuda and naga, *the emblem of King Rama II.*

Left: The interior.

Opposite
Top left: The west base of spire.

Middle left: The northern pediment bears the insignia of King Rama I, the Thai numeral one.

Top right: Below the pediments is the architectural detail known as the 'beehive' design, which is particular to the Rattanakosin period.

Below left: The west pediment with the insignia of King Rama III.

Detail showing the Order of the White Elephant.

Right: The doors and windows are topped with crown-like structures, rather than mondop-*style decoration. The gold lacquer doors are in lotus-bud pattern.*

Top and above: Details of the ceramic mosaic covering the exterior walls of Prasat Phra Thep Bidorn.

Left: The inner panel of the door frame with Thai decorations in gilded stucco.

Phra Mondop *(Library)* ❿

This building is situated to the rear of Prasat Phra Thep Bidorn on the same base. King Rama I ordered its construction to the north of the Ubosot to replace the former Phra Monthien Tham which was burnt. This earlier building had been constructed in the middle of a pond to prevent attack by termites – a common practice during the late Ayutthaya and early Bangkok period. Its purpose was to house the Tripitaka (Buddhist scriptures) which he had revised at Wat Mahathat in 1788 (the previous edition having been lost in the sack of Ayutthaya in 1767).

The library was extensively restored during the reign of King Rama III to commemorate the 50th anniversary of Bangkok. The cruciform building has a *mondop*-style roof. Originally it

Above: The south entrance. The exterior walls and columns are covered with green, silver and gold glass mosaic, with gilded stucco appliqué.

Left: One of the four replica Borobudur-style Buddhas which are placed at each of the four corners.

Below: Detail of the roof.

Opposite: Phra Mondop seen from the entrance of the temple compound. Note the mondop-style roof.

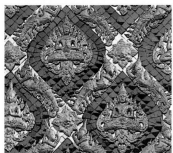

was on a higher base which raised it above the Ubosot. Accordingly when King Rama IV built Prasat Phra Thep Bidorn and Phra Sri Rattana Chedi, this building was seen to be too tall and was lowered.

The exterior walls are covered in glass mosaic in a lotus bud design, with green the predominant colour. Around the base is a row of stucco and gilded *devas* atop a row of *asuras* (giants) interspersed with *garudas*. The entrances are surmounted by *mondop*-style tops. The doors are inlaid with mother-of-pearl with a design of eight circles enclosing characters from the *Ramakien*. Characters include Pipek holding a club, Mangkorngun holding an arrow, Wayubudr holding a trident and a flag, Sukreep flying holding a sword, Pali holding a *kanok*, Ongkot flying, Phra Ram holding a sword, and a *hamsa* (sacred goose). At the base of the pillars are four sandstone Buddhas in Borobudur style. Those *in situ* are replicas but the originals may be seen in the Museum of the Emerald Buddha (38).

The steps leading up to the building have a *naga* balustrade. These *nagas* have a human face and are crowned. They date from the First Reign and are unique to this building. A pair of 175 cm gilded *asuras* stand on either side of each of the four doors. In their hands they hold clubs decorated with glass mosaic. Those on the north are both called Phraya Guwaychulart; on the south Phraya Tosatat; on the east Indrajit; on the west Phraya Balai.

The interior is not open to the public. A silver mat covers the floor. On a three-tiered base stands a large mother-of-pearl bookcase with a *mondop*-style top. It houses the 84,000 chapters of the Tripitaka. The upper tier of the base is decorated with a design of *theppanom* praying deities, the middle tier are *garudas* holding *nagas*, and the lower tier are *asuras* holding clubs.

Above: Running around the base of the Mondop is a row of small gilded stucco praying garudas *alternating with* asuras, *while above may be discerned the lower part of praying* devas.

Top: The large mother-of-pearl manuscript cabinet inside the Mondop stands on a silver mat.

Middle: The detail of the glass mosaic shows praying devas *with two* devatas.

Right: The upper tier of the base of the cabinet has a continuous frieze of small giants holding clubs.

Opposite: A corner of the Mondop showing the replica Buddha image.

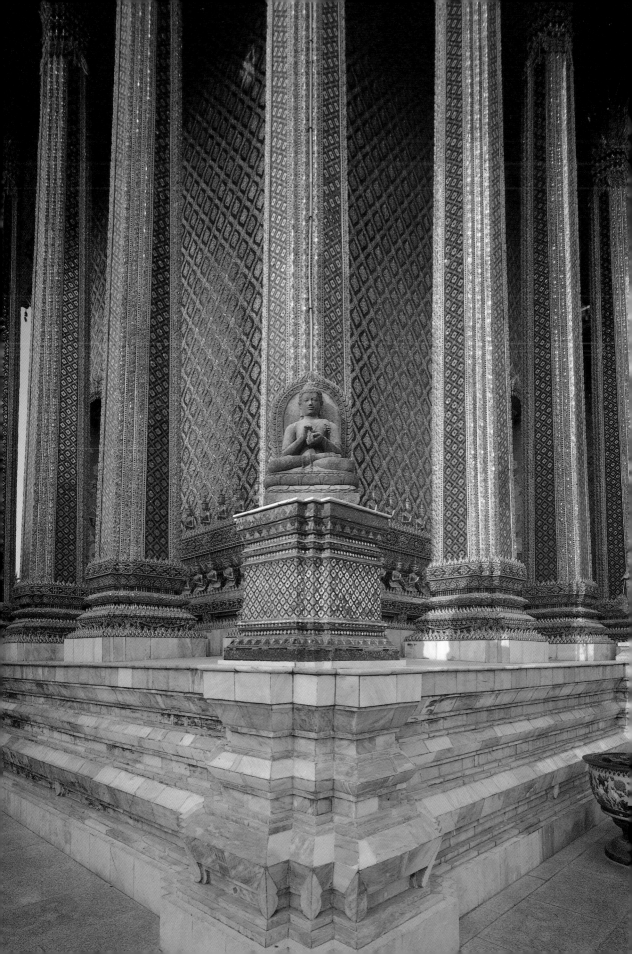

Below: The pediment of the chedi.

Opposite: Phra Sri Rattana Chedi.

Below right: The gold doors are decorated with the so-called 'falling flower' design in glass mosaic.

Phra Sri Rattana Chedi ⑪

This is situated behind the Mondop on the same base. King Rama IV ordered its construction in order to house a Buddha relic. His original plan, as mentioned above, was that the Emerald Buddha would be rehoused in Prasat Phra Thep Bidorn, with the Mondop housing the Buddhist scriptures behind it and this *stupa* at the back, thereby echoing the classic arrangement of *stupas* in a straight line which had been characteristic of Buddhist architecture since the Sukhothai and Ayutthaya period.

The bell-shape of the *chedi* is based on the larger ones at Wat Phra Sri Sanphet in Ayutthaya. On each of the four sectors of the circular base are four protruding porches allowing access to the interior. Miniature *chedis* are placed on top of the porches. The *chedi* is covered with gold mosaic which was added by King Rama V and was originally ordered from Italy. The mosaic has recently been replaced.

Inside is a circular room with another miniature *chedi* copying the larger one in black lacquer on a base. Tiered umbrellas hang down from the ceiling. It is not open to the public.

Apart from the major buildings discussed above, other smaller structures and sculptures adorn the raised terrace.

Two pairs of Decorated Chedis ⑫

It is believed that these were originally placed at each of the four corners of Mondop during the major restoration during the reign of King Rama III. However in the reign of King Rama IV and his construction of the large Phra Sri Rattana Chedi they were probably in the way and had to be relocated to their present position.

They have square, redented bases and are covered in gold leaf and glass mosaic. Although they are small, their proportions and decoration are of a high standard.

Replica of Angkor Wat ⑬

King Rama IV had the idea of moving one of the Khmer temples to Thailand as he thought the populace would be interested in seeing something unusual. However, having inspected various sites his officials informed him that they were far too large to move! Accordingly he ordered that a miniature replica be constructed to the north of the Mondop. The construction was only finished in the Fifth Reign.

Above: Detail of one of the four small chedis *decorated with gold leaf and glass* mosaic.

Right: Glittering glass mosaic on the small chedi.

Left: The replica of Angkor Wat, is behind Viharn Yod *(left) and* Ho Phra Monthien Tham *(right).*

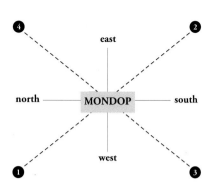

Right: The Monument to the First, Second and Third Reigns is combined.

Far right: The Monument to the Fourth Reign is one of the four Monuments of the Royal Insignia.

Phra Borom Ratchasanyarak
(Monuments of the Royal Insignia) ⓮

King Rama V, during the restoration of the Emerald Buddha Temple for the centenary of Bangkok in 1882, ordered the construction of three monuments, known in Thai as *busabok*, to display the royal insignia particular to the various reigns. In the present reign, the descendants of the various reigns presented funds for the construction of a fourth to display the insignia of the Sixth to Ninth Reigns.

The first *busabok* to the northwest of the Phra Mondop commemorates the first three reigns. That of King Rama I is represented by the Royal coat of arms and his own insignia of a Thai crown without the ear ornaments, King

Rama II by the *garuda* holding two *nagas* and King Rama III by a tripartite pavilion or flying palace.

The second *busabok* is reserved for King Rama IV and is represented by a Thai crown with ear ornaments.

The third *busabok* shows the insignia of King Rama V, the top part of the the Thai crown.

The fourth *busabok* displays the insignia of four reigns: King Rama VI is represented by a Vajra with lightning bolts; King Rama VII by three arrows; King Rama VIII by a Bodhisattva; and King Rama IX by the Octagonal Throne surmounted by a discus with the Thai numeral 9 inside and a seven-tiered Umbrella of State.

Each *busabok* stands on a two-tiered marble base with inscriptions relating to the kings and their building or repair work within the temple compound. Many bronze elephants stand on each of the four sides. These are meant to represent the white elephants associated with each reign.

Insignia of the Second Reign.

Insignia of the Fourth Reign.

Insignia of the Fifth Reign.

Insignia of the Sixth Reign.

Insignia of the Seventh Reign.

Insignia of the Eighth Reign.

Insignia of the Ninth Reign.

Mythological beings from the Himavamsa Forest ⑮

Seven pairs of various half-animal/half-celestial beings believed to inhabit this mythological forest are also dotted around the upper terrace. These include *Theppaksi* with the head of humans and bird bodies; *Thepnorasi*, half-lion half-male angel; *Apsarasingha*, female angel and lion; *Asurapaksi*, with head of a giant and lower body of a bird; *Kinnorn*, lower body of a bird and the top half of a man; *Asurawayupak*, lower body of a bird and head of an *asura*.

Left: Asurapaksi, the head of a giant and body of a bird (Asurawayupak).

Above: In the foreground stands a Kinnorn, which has the body of a man but with a bird's tail (Theppaksi).

Theppaksi.

Singhapasorn.

Thepnorasi.

Asurapaksi.

Kinnorn.

Asurawayupak.

Kinnorn.

Thepnorasi.

Apsarasingha.

The Southern Porch.

Southern porch ⓰

Various details indicate that this was probably a former entrance to the Mondop. The small pediment is decorated with a *viman*, or tripartite pavilion, the symbol of King Rama III, while the door panels are carved and gilded wood portraying a Chinese warrior holding a pike. The other side of the door has a multi-coloured Chinese-style design of birds in trees against a red background.

Western porch ⓱

From its style it has been deduced that this cruciform porch was probably constructed during the Fourth Reign contemporaneously with the raised terrace. The ceramic decoration is similar to that used on other buildings of this period. In the centre of the roof is a spire decorated with glass mosaic. The finial of the pediment which was usually a wooden *garuda*, has here been transformed into a stucco and ceramic *garuda's* head, in line with the taste of King Rama IV.

If no restoration is taking place, try to descend from the raised terrace by the north-eastern steps or by the ones you ascended.

Above: Pediment detail showing the insignia associated with the Third Reign.
Left: Carved and gilded Chinese warriors guard the doors.

Western Porch.

Detail of the Western Porch's door panels.

Above and left: The ceramic decoration of the Western Porch.

Ho Phra Nak *(The Royal Mausoleum)* ⑱

This is situated to the north of Phra Sri Rattana Chedi. It was originally constructed by King Rama I to house a Buddha image from Ayutthaya made of *nak* (gold mixed with copper), hence its name. It was also used to store the ashes of female members of the royal family in keeping with tradition handed down from Ayutthaya.

The building has been renovated in the various restorations, but the original Buddha image has been moved to the adjacent Viharn Yod. Today it is used to store the crematory relics of the Front Palace and the crematory relics of members of the royal family not of *Chao Fa* rank (*Chao Fa* meaning children begot by the king with a queen) or begot by kings with a consort or concubine. These relics are contained in hundreds of small urns.

The pediment has the frequently found *kanok* motif whose ends terminate in *theppanom*. Low steps on either side lead to a marble terrace in front of the single entrance with a *mondop*-style door surround. The window frames have double *naga* surrounds.

Ho Phra Nak.
Below left: Detail of the pediment.
Below right: The eave brackets.

Viharn Yod ⑲

This is situated next to Ho Phra Nak. Formerly it housed a silver Buddha image which was cast by King Rama I from various religious deities previously belonging to King U-Thong, founder of Ayutthaya in 1351. These had been destroyed by the Burmese in the first sack of the capital in 1753.

King Rama III had it rebuilt and installed the *nak* Buddha image from Ho Phra Nak, together with other important Buddha images.

Above: Detail showing the Jor Por Ror *initials of King Rama V above the windows of Viharn Yod.*

Top: Looking across to Viharn Yod from the raised terrace.

The cruciform building has longer arms to the north and south. The stucco spire is in the form of a Thai crown and is in stucco decorated with Chinese porcelain. It is one of the finest examples of such a spire in Rattanakosin architecture. The porcelain came from dishes and plates broken in transit and fashioned into flowers. It is similar to the *kratong* made of fresh flowers and banana leaves, presented as offerings to sacred objects. Ceramic is used through out and thus the finials and *chofa,* tradionally made

The porcelain chofa *is in the form of a* garuda's *head.*

made from wood, were changed to plaster covered with porcelain. The *chofa,* which in wood are highly stylized, are here more representational. Porcelain also decorates the redented corners, the structural pilasters and the window surrounds. The *Jor Por Ror* insignia indicates that the building was restored in the Fifth Reign.

On either side of the steps on the east and west sides stand a pairs of bronze sculptures of Tantima birds, whose bodies are normal birds but whose heads are *garudas.* The mother-of-pearl inlaid doors on the north should also be noted, as the quality of their workmanship may be compared with the central door of the Ubosot itself. These date from the reign of King Borommakot of Ayutthaya (r.1732-1758) and were taken from Wat Pa Mok in Ang Tong district.

If you wish to start studying the Ramakien murals around the cloisters, the first and last rooms are here.

Detail of the mother-of-pearl doors.

The mother-of-pearl inlay doors on the north side of Viharn Yod.

Above: One of the small Chinese lions at the base of the steps.

Four top pictures: Details of the intricate porcelain patterning covering the pediment, corners, finials and base of Viharn Yod.

Left: One of the two small stone giants guarding the top of the steps.

Far left: Bronze Tantima bird.

Top: Ho Phra Monthien Tham.

Above: Five theppanom *occupy the niches below the pediment.*

Top: Ho Phra Monthien Tham.

Ho Phra Monthien Tham *(The Supplementary Library)* 20

This building is situated to the east of Viharn Yod. King Rama I had it constructed to house various versions of the Buddhist Scriptures and as a building where monks and novices could sit their exams. The deputy King sent workmen from his palace to help in the construction and accordingly the building has many particular features. Currently it is used to house certain mother-of-pearl inlay cabinets and for sermons on Buddhist Holy Days.

The rectangular building has a lower tiered roof at the front and back. The pediment has the unusual iconography of Brahma mounted on *hamsa* at the top, above Phra Isuan (Indra) on his elephant Erawan (Airavata) below, against a background of *kanok* terminating in *theppanom*.

The panel below the pediment is also unusual, with the normal pierced foliage decoration being replaced with small *theppanom* in five arched niches and foliage below. The door surround of the central door is in *mondop* style.

The mother-of-pearl inlaid doors from Wat Boromaputharam in Ayutthaya date to King Borommakot's reign. The windows and secondary doors flanking the main door are surrounded by a double *naga* frame while the actual frames have infills in the top corners carved with a monkey on either side. These can be compared with window frames in the National Museum which was formerly the Front Palace.

Although this building is not open to the public, on Buddhist Holy Days when sermons are being preached, Thai Buddhists can enter and foreigners may glimpse the interior. Above the windows are four rows of celestial beings painted against red and black backgrounds known as *thep chumnum*. These are the only mural paintings in the whole complex to reflect the influence of Ayutthaya. Between the windows are pairs of male and female deities. The inside of the window panels show sword-bearing deities on stands borne by monkeys.

Above: Brahma on hamsa, *above Indra on (Erawan) from the pediment of Ho Phra Monthien Tham.*

Top left: The central mother-of-pearl doors of Ho Phra Monthien Tham.

Top right: Detail of the doors.

From here walk past two giants with cockerel-plumed crowns, *Mayarap* (J) and *Virunchambang* (I), and on along the west wall of the compound to another pair of giants, *Sahasadeja* (K) and *Tosakanth* (L), before walking along the length of the Ubosot again and past the entrance to see the last few structures with the complex.

Above: *Gandhara Buddha Viharn taken during the Fifth Reign showing that at one time two white giants stood in front of the entrance.*

Top right: *Gandhara Buddha Viharn and Yod Prang Mondop. In the front may be seen the small porch over one of the pairs of Sema stones which surround the Emerald Buddha Temple.*

Top left: *Porcelain* naga *finials and pediment.*

Gandhara Buddha Viharn and Yod Prang Mondop ㉑

Both these buildings stand on the same base and are situated to the south-east of the Ubosot. They were built on the order of King Rama IV. The *viharn* was built for the installation of the Gandhara Buddha used in the Royal Ploughing Ceremony and the Rain-making Ceremony, while the *mondop* to its rear was to house a northern-style *chedi* which King Mongkut obtained while he was still a prince and monk during the reign of King Rama III. The practice of situating a *viharn* with a Buddha image and a *stupa* behind with a relic was common during the Sukhothai and Ayutthaya periods so that worshippers could pay respects to both at the same time.

The roofs of both these buildings are topped with Khmer-style *prangs* in stucco decorated with porcelain whose form is more elongated than usual. The porch of the Gandhara Viharn is in Thai style with *chofa* in the shape of a *garuda* and finials in the form of *naga* heads. The pediment is decorated with porcelain flowers and foliage. The walls of the building are clad in yellow, green and navy porcelain tiles which were the first to be made in Thailand rather than imported. Other interesting feature are the windows and doors decorated with sheaves of rice and fishes and shrimps, signifying the fecundity of the rice fields. Around the building stand stone Chinese lions.

Above: The doors and windows are carved with gilded rice sheaves.

Above left: This northern-style chedi *was acquired by King Mongkut while he was still a monk.*

Left: Interior of Gandhara Buddha Viharn with the Buddha image used in the Royal Ploughing Ceremony.

Above: Detail and two views of the Belfry as rebuilt by King Rama IV.

The Belfry 🟢

This is situated to the south of the Ubosot and was built by King Rama I at the same time as the Ubosot in order to house a large bell. According to the principles of Buddhist architecture, the structures within a temple should include an Ubosot for the monks to perform religious ceremonies, a *viharn* to house various Buddha images, a *mondop* for storing the Buddhist scriptures, *chedis* for housing sacred relics or images and a belfry to sound the time for ceremonies, prayers, etc. Thus, although the Emerald Buddha Temple is not residential and therefore the belfry has probably not been much used, its presence is necessary in order to fulfil the requirements of Buddhist architecture.

The current belfry was rebuilt by King Rama IV on the original site and only completed during the reign of King Rama V to celebrate the centenary of Bangkok. The bell came from either Wat Rakheng or was created during the First Reign.

The entire structure is covered in Chinese porcelain in floral and geometric patterns with double *naga* frames over the doors. The spire is in *mondop* style. The base is in two tiers with the bottom part being redented on all four sides. There are doors on all four sides.

Ho Rajbongsanusorn 🟢, Phra Photithat Piman 🟢, Ho Rajkoramanusorn 🟢

These three small structures constructed in the Fourth Reign, adjoin the low wall to the west of the Ubosot with Ho Rajkoramanusorn to the north, Phra Photithat Piman in the middle and Ho Rajbongsanusorn to the south. They are just behind the hermit you saw upon entering the compound. Ho Phra Rajbongsanusorn was to house Buddha images in the various attitudes corresponding to the king in particular reigns. Ho Rajkoramanusorn houses some 37 Buddha images representing each of the various reigns of Ayutthaya and Thonburi, while the middle building houses a small *stupa* which Prince Mongkut (later King Rama IV) obtained from the north while he was still a prince. It houses a Buddha relic.

The Buddha images housed within the two pavilions are small in size. King Rama III ordered the casting of 37 of these using bronze from Juntuk district in Khorat province. King Rama IV ordered bases for them all and had them gold plated. 34 inscriptions were added to commemorate the kings of Ayutthaya and Thonburi, with the remaining three being dedicated to

Kings Rama I, II and III. Subsequent kings followed the tradition so that now there 8 dedicated to the kings of the Chakri dynasty.

The two rectangular pavilions are similar in size and decoration, with the only differences being the four pediments which bear the insignia of the first four Chakri kings. The window and door surrounds give the appearance of being in traditional Thai style but in fact there are important differences in the detail such as in the leaves surrounding the frame, or in the flowers in the small pediments above the windows which are Chinese in style.

Phra Photithat Piman, The central structure is in the form of a *busabok* or Thai throne with a crown-style spire.

Having examined this last group of buildings, you should now exit the building through the southern Srirattana Sasada Gate, guarded by two giants with small elephant trunks instead of noses. Totkiritorn is red and Totkirijun is dark green.

Behind the rishi *where you first came in are three small structures, from left to right: Ho Rajkoramanusorn, Phra Photithat Piman and Ho Rajbongsanusorn.*

Pediment of Ho Rajkoramanusorn.

Pediment of Ho Rajbongsanusorn.

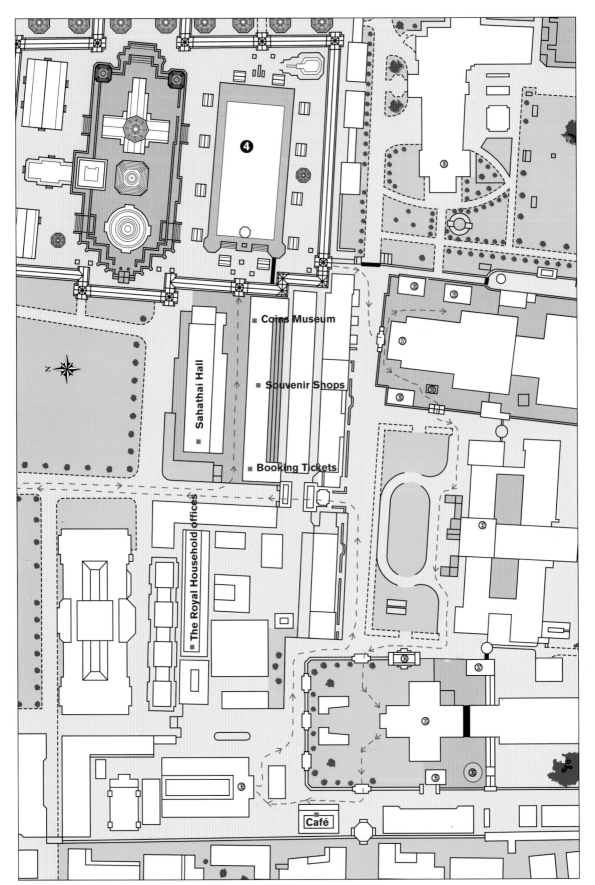

Coins Museum

Souvenir Shops

Booking Tickets

Sahathai Hall

The Royal Household offices

Café

N

Central Court: The Throne Halls and Royal Residences

Having left the area of the Emerald Buddha temple you will now pass into the Central Court of the Grand Palace, formerly the royal residence of the Chakri kings until the end of the Sixth Reign. The two areas are divided by the Amornwithi Road. Today many of the main throne halls are still used for important ceremonies. Several significant buildings are not visitable by the general public but some photographs are included so that the visitor can gain an impression of the whole. These are shown against a cream background.

Opposite: Plan of the Central Court.

Below: Looking across the Sivalai Garden, toward Mahisorn Maha Prasat from the Sitaraphirom Pavilion. In the left middle ground may be seen Phra Buddha Rattanasathan.

Above: A stone Chinese sculpture from inside the courtyard of the Phra Thinang Amarin Winichai.

Top: The rear facade of Phra Thinang Boromphiman.

As you walk towards the Phra Maha Monthien group pause at the wrought iron gates to look at the west of Phra Thinang Boromphiman.

Phra Thinang Boromphiman ㉖

Constructed in the reign of King Rama V between 1897-1903 this building is not open to the public. The two storey building was designed by and built under the supervision of a foreign architect in neo-Renaissance style. Thai decorative details can be found only on the walls and front porch, which was the first to be designed for a carriage to enter. It is used as accomodation for royal visitors.

Looking in a southerly direction, you will see the Dusit Sasadar Gate topped by a four-headed Brahma. Formerly this gate was used by ladies of the Inside to reach the Emerald Buddha Temple. Visitors cannot pass through this gate and should retrace their steps to visit the the Phra Maha Monthien Group formerly the royal residence of Kings Rama I to Rama VI. Turn right and then turn left through the entrance porch in grey marble, decorated on the top with Chinese porcelain. Four Chinese stone guardians stand guard.

Phra Maha Monthien group

This group of buildings, surrounded by a stucco wall, is composed of three important halls: the Phra Thinang Chakraphat Phiman, Phra Thinang Phaisan Thaksin and Phra Thinang Amarin Winichai. These together with various smaller edifices formed the royal residence for the first four Chakri kings. All are in traditional Thai style. Today the Phra Maha Monthien Group is still used for important ceremonies such as the Coronation and the Assumption of the Palace Ceremony at the beginning of each reign. It is also considered particularly sacred because it houses the *deva* Phra Sayam Devadhiraj who is considered to watch over the welfare of the country.

Enter by the Thewaphiban gate. Within the complex, only one third of the buildings can be seen by the general public and of those only Phra Thinang Amarin Winichai can be entered.

Below: The architecture in the Phra Maha Monthien Group varies in style. The entrance gate to the Inner Court is surmounted by a Khmer-style prang-shaped spire. Typical Thai-style buildings were used to house Buddha images, while the steps leading to the gallery in front of the Ho Phra Sulalai are in Chinese style.

Interiors of the Phra Maha Monthien Group

Two thirds of the buildings in the Phra Maha Monthien form part of the Inner Court and as such are unvisitable by the general public. However as they play an important role in royal ritual and ceremonies, a brief description is in order:

Phra Thinang Phaisan Thaksin.

This Phra Thinang is directly behind and connected with Phra Thinang Amarin Winichai. Built during the First Reign, it was used by King Rama I for dining, relaxation and merit making. Since his death it has become a tradition that the new king receives the invitation to rule over the kingdom in this hall. Two thrones are used during the coronation ceremonies *(see page 135)*. In the middle of this hall is the altar of Phra Sayam Devadhiraj, the symbolic guardian of the country, installed by King Rama IV. Two Ho Phra (chapels) flank this throne hall: the Ho Phra Sulalai Phiman to the east, housing important Buddha images and sacred objects; the Ho Phra That Monthien, housing the crematory relics of the first three Chakri kings to the west.

Phra Thinang Chakraphat Phiman.

This is the main building of the group and was the residence of the all Chakri kings, some spending the whole reign in residence, some spending a few nights. The Assumption of the Palace Ceremony is an intergal part of the Coronation Ceremony as the kings all proclaim that residence in the palace of their forefathers.

The annexes on the right and the left that flank the inner audience hall served as living quarters for the queen and court ladies. King Rama VI named them the Phra Thinang Thep Sathanphilat and the Phra Thinang Theppa-atphilai.

Interior of Phra Thinang Phaisan Thaksin. The Phra Sayam Devadhiraj altar is to the left, while at the back on the right is the octagonal throne used during the coronation.

*The Bhadrapitha Coronation Throne is surmounted
by a white nine-tiered umbrella.*

*The central section of the Phra Thinang Chakraphat Phiman.
The mural shows the assembly of the multitude of the* devas.

*The royal bedstead as used by King Rama I. The underneath
of the nine-tiered umbrella is just visible above the bed.*

*At the back of the veranda in front of the Ho Phra That Monthien
is the low table-like throne used by King Rama IV if emergencies
arose during the night.*

Phra Thinang Amarin Winichai 🟡

This is the most important throne hall in the Phra Maha Monthien complex because it is the formal audience hall where every Chakri king has performed important state ceremonies, such as making his appearance before his subjects during the coronation ceremony, conducting audiences with ministers of state, performing rites on his birthday, and receiving the credentials of foreign ambassadors. It was here that King Rama II, seated on the magnificent Busabok Maha Mala Throne, an open-pillared construction of wood with a multi-tiered roof, received the British envoy, John Crawfurd, sent to Siam by the Governor-General of India to conduct trade negotiations.

The large throne hall stands on a 50 cm high base. The roof is covered in green and orange tiles and has the customary *chofa* finials decorated with glass mosaic and gold leaf. The central pediment shows Amarin Thirat seated in a tripartite palace against *kanok* foliage, while the carved wood side pediments have flower motifs, in-filled with glass mosaic.

The window and door surrounds are in stucco covered with gold leaf and glass mosaic, topped with small double pediments. The outside of the window panels have a flower design in black and gold lacquer, while the insides are painted with *devas* holding swords and standing on a base. The entrance door has a lacquer design of lotus buds. The inner panels of the door depict standing demons holding weapons in their capacity as guardians of the deities who protect the Phra Maha Monthien; the only place in the Grand Palace where demons serve as door guardians.

Left: King Rama V taking his ceremonial bath during the Record Reign Anniversary in 1908. Note the Brahmans standing in the foreground (RBC).

Far left: The porch over the steps leading to the gallery in front of the Ho Phra Sulalai is in Chinese style. On both sides of the porch are false windows adorned with stucco reliefs in Western style. To the left are some columns of the Phra Thinang Ratcharuedee. To the right is a wall of Phra Thinang Amarin Winichai.

Above: The Phra Thawan
Thewaphiban entrance to the
Phra Thinang Amarin
Winichai, has three gates. The
middle one reserved for the
king is correspondingly more
imposing; those on either side
were for government officials
and the public. This was built
at the same time as the wall
around the Phra Maha
Monthien in the reign of King
Rama IV. The edges of the
pediments, capitals, and
pillars are decorated with
Chinese ceramics. Chinese
stone statues guard the
entrance.

Opposite: The two thrones
within the Phra Thinang
Amarin Winichai, with the
boat-shaped Busabok Maha
Mala Chakraphat Phiman
throne behind, and the
Phuttan Kanchanasinghat
Throne in front.

Inside the audience hall are two parallel rows of five huge square pillars of stucco-covered brick painted with small flower and foliage motifs on a gold background. The coffered ceiling is decorated with gold and glass mosaic stars typical of the early Rattanakosin period.

The two intricately carved wooden thrones date from the reign of King Rama I. The lower, square throne in front is the Phra Racha Bunlang which has gilded *garudas* and *devas* surrounding the base. It is surmounted with a nine-tiered white umbrella on the occasion of the Grand Audience. The Phuttan Kanchanasinghat throne is placed on top with the Crown of Victory and the Betel Nut Set. Behind stands the boat-shaped Busabok Maha Mala Chakraphat Phiman throne, which elaborately gilded and decorated with glass mosaic, rests on a gilded masonry dais surrounded by wooden *deva* figures. Four pillars support the superstructure of the throne. The elevated dias, which was constructed by King Rama III, represents Mount Meru. The top level is decorated with *garudas* holding *naga*.

Above: Ho Sastrakhom, which was restored during the reign of King Rama IV

(Phra Thinang Racharuedee is visible behind.)

Ho Sastrakhom 28

Situated to the east of Phra Thinang Amarin Winichai is a small building attached to the wall. Here Mon monks would chant over the lustral water used to sprinkle and bless the Grand Palace. During times of war, the potency of weapons were enhanced in a special ceremony and amulets were presented to soldiers to protect them in battle. As a result of this latter function the windows and doors of this hall depict ancient weapon designs.

Phra Thinang Racharuedee 29

Several small buildings have borne this name since the reign of King Rama IV. This cruciform open pavilion, built during the reign of King Rama VI, measures 12 x 7.80 metres. The pediments are decorated with a gilded Phra Narai on *garuda* against a background of white glass mosaic. The white marble base protrudes on two sides. The west side is used during ceremonies which require the king partake of a ceremonial shower before the ceremony begins and on completion of each twelve-year cycle. The north side of the protruding marble base is used for making offerings to *devas*.

Dusidaphirom Pavilion ㉚

Projecting from the north-west corner of the wall surrounding the Phra Maha Monthien group this pavilion on a high base was originally open on all sides. King Rama III added the walls, which are painted with gold and black lacquer, both inside and out. The pavilion was then used as a robing chamber for the king when arriving and departing by palanquin or elephant, hence the elephant-mounting platform on the west exterior of the wall and the palanquin one on the north; on the east side steps lead down to the courtyard in front of Phra Thinang Amarin Winichai. The pediments are decorated with *devas* holding swords. The exterior walls are painted in the *kanok* pattern on a pale green background, making this building the only remaining one whose walls are painted. The interior has two rows of four octagonal columns, again decorated in the *kanok* pattern, this time gold on black. The upper part of the interior walls are painted with *devas*, *yakshas* and humans, while the lower part has trees with birds.

Sanam Chan Pavilion ㉛

This is the only building in traditional Thai style to be built in the Central Court of the Grand Palace in the reign of King Rama II, who used the pavilion for relaxing while supervising construction projects. Being small (3.30 x 4.50m) it was portable and could move to different sites. The wooden pediments decorated with gilded wood carvings and glass mosaic are particularly fine, fusing floral and foliage motifs in Chinese and Western styles. The eight columns are gilded and inlaid with glass mosaic. The base of the raised inner dais is decorated with black lacquer and glass mosaic, topped with a single teak panel measuring 1.50 x 2 metres.

Above: Sanamrachakit Gate is one of the entrances to the Inner court.

Top right: The Sanam Chan Pavilion combines the superb proportions of traditional Thai architecture and exquisite decoration.

Top left: The Dusidaphirom Pavilion was originally used for relaxation and merit-making ceremonies.

Exit the Phra Maha Monthien complex via the Thevesraksa Gate. Glancing to your left you will see another gate, the Sanamrachakit Gate. This gate leads to the Inside, formerly housing the residences of the Queens, wives and concubines, children and female attendants. This area was prohibited to all those without permission and in particular was barred to men. Even today all men have to ask for special permission. The gate is open from 6.00 to 18.00 every day. On the outside a soldier stands guard, while inside is a female guard who habitually passes the time by making flower garlands. After peering through the gate, turn around and approach the Phra Thinang Chakri Maha Prasat Throne fronted with a lawn and various ornamental trees.

Above: A stucco guardian stands inside the entrance to the passageway leading to Phra Thinang Phaisan Thaksin. On the right a woman can be seen making garlands.

Right and middle: A group of royal ladies relaxing in one of the salons and the garden of the Inner Court.

Below: The all-female band of the Inner Court.

The Chakri Maha Prasat Group

Royal Buildings in the Fifth Reign

Having grown up in the Grand Palace, when Prince Chulalongkorn ascended the throne as King Rama V he decided to build a new group of as residences for himself and the royal family. His mother's residence was demolished and the construction of several connecting large *Phra Thinangs* was initiated. Building began in 1868 and continued until 1870, whereupon the buildings were given the following names: Phra Thinang Mul Sathan Boroma-at, Phra Thinang Sommotti Thewarat Upbat, Phra Thinang Damrong Sawat Ananwong, and Phra Thinang Pipat Pong Thaworn Wijid. In addition, there were two *Ho* (small buildings, one to house Buddha images and the other relics of former kings) in accordance with the architectural traditions associated with royal residence complexes or *Phra Racha Monthien.*

Before these buildings were completed, King Rama V travelled to Singapore and Java. Upon his return he ordered the construction of another *Phra Thinang* behind the four mentioned above. This was large and long and was called Phra Thinang Barommaraj Satid Maholarn. The whole was surrounded by a castellated wall. The king took up residence in Phra Thinang Mul Sathan Boroma-at in 1873.

In 1875, just as his father King Rama IV had done before him, King Rama V decided to build a throne hall to house the royal tiered umbrella and to receive important guests. Formerly in the Phra Thinang Chakrapat Phiman group, Phra Thinang Amarin Winichai had served as the throne hall, while the Fourth Reign's Phra Thinang Ananda Samakhom was used for receiving guests and foreign ambassadors. The new throne hall was in front of the Phra Thinang Mul Sathan Boroma-at and the Phra Thinang Sommotti Thewarat Upbat. John Clunich from England was the chief architect, while Henry Clunich Rose was his assistant. The king had seen their work in Singapore where John Clunich had designed Government House. On the Thai side, Phraya Bhanuwong Mahakosathibodi was Director of Construction. The foundation stone was laid on 7 May 1876 and the building was completed in 1882 in time to celebrate both the Racha Monthien group and the centenary of the founding of Bangkok and the Chakri dynasty. Accordingly the new *Phra Thinang* was named Phra Thinang Chakri Maha Prasat.

After the king had moved to his new residence, between 1882 and 1887, he ordered the construction of a further four *Phra Thinang* behind Phra Thinang Barommaraj Satid Maholarn, namely Phra Thinang Amorn Phiman Manee as a palace for sleeping, Phra Thinang Suttara Sri Aphirom as a residence for Queen Saowabha, Phra Thinang Bannakom Sorani as a library and Phra Thinang Racha Pridi Warotai as a sitting room. In addition, he also ordered the creation of a garden on the roof of the building used as a treasury as well as a garden at the same level as his residence, naming this Suan Sawan or Heavenly Garden. From this latter garden a bridge connected to the residence of Queen Sawang Vadhana. During this reign many residences were built for the royal consorts and the concentration of buildings blocked the breeze, making roof terrraces almost a necessity.

King Rama V lived in this complex until the latter part of his reign when in around 1900 he began living in the recently-built Dusit Palace in north Bangkok. However he did not immediately abandon the Grand Palace but moved between the two. Only at the very end of his reign did the king use the Grand Palace as a residence solely when royal ceremonies were in progress. He died at Phra Thinang Amphorn Satan, Dusit Palace on 23 October 1910.

The Sixth to Ninth Reigns

Following his accession to the throne, King Rama VI only resided in the Phra Maha Chakri group occasionally. Rather, the king liked to stay in several different palaces, both in Bangkok and in the country.

By the reign of King Rama VII (1926-1935), the various *Phra Thinang* were somewhat delapidated and in need of restoration. However as this was a time of economic depression there were only sufficient funds for the renovation of Phra Thinang Chakri Maha Prasat under the direction of Prince Iddhidebsarn Kritakara, an architectural graduate of the Ecole des Beaux Arts in Paris. The results of his work may still be seen today.

In the present reign, the other *Phra Thinang* which had lacked restoration for many years were of necessity demolished. Only Phra Thinang Mul Sathan Boroma-at and Phra Thinang Sommotti Thewarat Upbat were reconstructed on their old sites and with a replica of their original decoration. Behind these buildings the open area was turned into a lawn. More recently, construction of a new *Phra Thinang* has been started here once more in order to hold state banquets.

Phra Thinang Chakri Maha Prasat photographed in the early 1900s.

Phra Thinang Chakri Maha Prasat ③

The lower part of this throne hall is built in neo-French Renaissance style but with tiered roofs and spires in traditional Thai style. Originally the roof was to have been domed but the Regent requested that Thai style should be used in order to match with the existing two throne halls on the same axis, thereby referring back to the former royal palace in Ayutthaya. In addition, in former reigns a *prasat* was traditionally built to glorify the king and this reign should be no exception. The throne hall is camposed of three pavilions or sections, which in Thai architectural terminology are considered as three separate *Phra Thinang*. It is not open to the public, but, owing to its importance, salient features of the interior are described in the box on pages 112-113.

Above: Mosaic portrait of King Rama V, on the lower porch.

Top: Phra Thinang Chakri Maha Prasat, showing the central portico with its blend of western and Thai architecture. Note the seven-tiered spire appropriate to a Maha Prasat.

Architectural features

Owing to the mix of western and Thai styles, the Thai elements are not arranged in as strict a fashion as normal. Thus there are tiered roofs on all three of the sections and these are all the same height; the roofs slant less than usual to take account of the large size of the building; the *chofa* are fatter and shorter than usual.

The state emblem under a crown.

The upper pediment of Phra Thinang Chakri Maha Prasat bears the emblem of State.

Right: The lower pediment of Phra Thinang Chakri Maha Prasat bears the emblem of the Chakri Dynasty.

Opposite: One of the two stairways leading to the entrance to Phra Thinang Chakri Maha Prasat. Note the bronze elephant, one of the pair guarding the stairway.

This latter feature was to minimize the fact that Phra Thinang Chakri Maha Prasat is a three-storey building amidst several one-storey buildings, albeit on raised bases, and to ensure that it blended harmoniously with its surroundings.

Other architectural details also depart from tradition. Thus the pediments of the two flanking pavilions which one might expect to find decorated with Phra Narai on *garuda*, or a *deva* with a sword, are instead decorated with the royal insignia of the Fifth Reign consisting of a crown on a *paan* (circular offering tray) carried by the three-headed elephant Erawan and flanked with a lion and a *Kojasi*. The central pediment is adorned with the emblem of state specific to the Fifth Reign: the Chakri symbol of a three-pronged fork and discus below a crown, with a shield containing the three-headed elephant Erawan, above another elephant and a pair of crossed daggers. On the pediment above the entrance porch on the first floor is the Chakri emblem surrounded by a chain, while on the curved pediment below the balcony railing is an mosaic portrait of King Chulalongkorn. Apart from the pediments, the Chakri emblem appears elsewhere on the building such as on the wrought iron gates *(see page 16)*.

The throne hall is entered on the first floor via a large porch projecting from the central part of the building. The porch may be approached by one of two staircases which rise up on either side. At the time when the throne hall was built early in the Fifth Reign, Thai architectural beliefs decreed that a staircase on the interior was inauspicious.

The Interior

The central section of the top floor of the throne hall houses the crematory relics of Kings Rama IV to VIII and the queens from the Fourth, Fifth and Seventh Reigns. The eastern wing houses important Buddha images and ceremonial offerings used by the king, while the western wing contains the crematory relics of other royal consorts and certain members of the royal family. In this reign following the cremation of the king's mother in 1997, her crematory relics were enshrined in a miniature urn together with those of the king's father. In addition, on this floor at the front is a special window where the king has occasionally appeared to his subjects.

The first floor is the most important. Upon entering, the visitor passes into the Front Audience Hall and from there straight on to the Central Throne Hall, or turning left to the Eastern Gallery or right to the Western Gallery, which in turn open onto reception halls used during royal banquets. In addition, the Eastern Gallery serves as a reception hall for ambassadors before they present their credentials to the king. The reception areas are decorated with portraits of the Chakri kings and queens, various carved thrones and bronze busts of members of European royal houses.

The Central Throne Hall, the most important part of the *phra thinang,* is where the king receives ambassadors, gives audiences on his birthday and holds state banquets for visiting kings and presidents. At the rear of the throne hall in front of an arched niche stands the Phuttanthom throne on a muti-tiered marble dais, sheltered by a nine-tiered white umbrella and flanked on either side by seven-tiered white umbrellas over the figure of a *deva* holding the king's sword, and the royal signet casket flanked by figures of a lion and a *kojasi.* The long side walls are hung with paintings of past diplomatic missions: Louis XIV's reception of the mission sent by King Narai the Great of Ayutthaya, the reception by Queen Victoria of King Rama IV's ambassador, the reception at Fontainbleau of a Siamese mission to Emperor Napoleon III, and King Rama IV's reception of the French Envoy at the Aphinaoniwet Group.

His Majesty King Bhumibol Adulyadej.

Above and opposite: The Central Throne Hall of Phra Thinang Chakri Maha Prasat. The photograph opposite was taken on the occasion of a banquet held to celebrate King Rama V's return from Europe in 1908.

Right: Her Majesty Queen Sirikit.

The Eastern Gallery has portraits of the kings of the Chakri dynasty. The busts are of members of European royal houses presented by them to King Rama V.

The Western Gallery with portraits of various queens of the Chakri dynasty. Note the thrones arranged around the walls.

A sao hong, or decorative column, in front of Phra Thinang Dusit Maha Prasat. This column from the Fourth Reign shows Mon influence.

Dusit Maha Prasat Group

The main building in this area of the Grand Palace dates from the First Reign. However, as with other parts of the Grand Palace various additions and embellishments have been made over successive reigns. Contained within a spacious walled and paved area is one major throne hall which is open to the public and a more private hall behind which is not. These are in turn surrounded by various less important buildings and open pavilions. Phra Thinang Dusit Maha Prasat was built to a cruciform plan topped with a beautiful *prasat*-style roof with soaring spire to glorify King Rama I and was used by him for important ceremonies and formal audiences when the king resided in the Dusit Maha Prasat group. On the northern side is an open-sided porch with throne which the king would use for royal audiences. Upon the king's death, the *phra thinang* was used for the lying-in-state and it has become the custom to place the remains of kings, queens and high-ranking members of the royal family there. The rear of the building connects with Phra Thinang Phiman Rattaya where the king used to sleep, with two simple structures on either side known as Phra Brat Sai and Phra Brat Kwa which were used by royal consorts and female members of the royal family. In the courtyard at the front on either side of Phra Thinang Dusit Maha Prasat are two *salas,* or L-shaped pavillions known as Tim Kod, constructed for courtiers and officials when the king made appearances on the throne in the porch.

Entrance to this area is through one of the three gates decorated with Chinese porcelain in floral patterns. These were added during the Fourth Reign. Also in this reign was added Phra Thinang Aporn Phimok Prasat, a small sala built on the eastern wall of the compound for use during various ceremonies. In the Fifth Reign, the king ordered the construction of Phra Thinang Rachakaranya Sapha on the eastern wall behind Phra Thinang Aporn Phimok Prasat for holding meetings with his ministers. In the Sixth Reign a hall for Plueng Krueng, as part of the royal funeral rites, was built on the west wall.

Phra Thinang Dusit Maha Prasat ㉝

This magnificent throne hall may be taken as an archetype of traditional Thai architecture within the Grand Palace, with every element proclaiming in symbolic form the majesty of the king based on Brahmanic ideas and those derived from Mahayana Buddhism. Thus the spire represents Mount Meru or in fact the universe of the gods.

The superstructure can be divided into three sections. The lower section is formed from seven superimposed tiers. Each tier, representing the various levels of heaven according to the beliefs of the Traiphum or Buddhist cosmology, has small gilded pediments on each side, with elements called *naga pak* on the redented corners. The middle section is in the form of a bell whose roundness has been flattened into a four-sided element representing the *stupa* in which the Buddha's ashes were interred. The top section is similar to the finial on a *chedi* composed of the *haem,* the lotus bud, the *pli,* the crystal and dew drop signifying the escape from *samsara* or rebirth.

The spire is supported by *garudas* on all four sides and these symbolise the mythical animals within the Himavamsa forest surrounding Mount Meru. The *garudas* wear full regalia and crowns. Their feet stand on *nagas* while their hands hold their tails.

The tiered roofs and spire of Phra Thinang Dusit Maha Prasat.

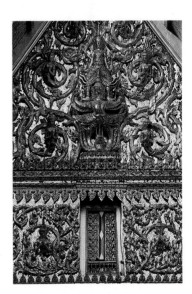

Above: The pediment depicts Phra Narai on garuda.

Opposite: The Dusit Maha Prasat has a Greek cross floor plan but a Thai-style superstructure. Note the open-sided porch on the side. As it is a Maha Prasat, the surrounds of the doors and windows are adorned in the prasat *form in accordance with Thai architectural tradition.*

The pediments are decorated with Phra Narai on *garuda*, a representation we have frequently encountered in the Grand Palace and symbolising the king's association with Phra Narai, who in human form descended to help humans and relieve them from suffering. Any building with such a motif on the pediment shows that it is a building associated with the monarch. In addition all the usual accoutrements of the pediment are there including *chofa* (head of the *garuda*), *bairaka* (*garuda*'s wings), *hang hong* (*naga*'s head) and *naga sadung*. The eave supports are in the form of *nagas* with lowered heads, symbolising the *naga* in its role as protector of the Buddha, here protecting the entrance used by the king.

The window and door surrounds are in the form of mini *prasats* and represent the *prasats* of the *devas* who protect the throne hall. The *phra thinang* stands on a high base with convex and concave mouldings, whose bottom layer, according to Thai belief, resembles the foot of a lion, hence the name lion base. This, like many of the symbolic references, is derived from India and the close association of the lion with the family of the Buddha.

The unusual feature of the throne hall is the small porch at the front of the building, whose pediment is another Phra Narai on *garuda*. Within the porch stands the Busabok Mala Throne whose spire echoes in miniature that of the main building. The base is surrounded with carved praying deities. During the First Reign, the throne was used when the king appeared before his vassal states, then later for certain ceremonies. Recently, during the celebrations for the bi-centenary of Bangkok, the Phra Sayam Devadhiraj guardian figure was placed here for the populace to come and pay their respects.

The lying-in-state of King Rama V within Phra Thinang Dusit Maha Prasat, 1910.

Interior

The walls are painted with a lotus bud design arranged geometrically across the wall and within the lotus bud is seated a praying deity – a motif which in Thai decorative tradition is associated with the most sacred places. The ceiling, which has a coffered octagonal section underneath the spire, is decorated with gilded and glass mosaic star-shaped motifs, to reinforce the impression of being in a heavenly realm. The interior panels of the window shutters are painted with pairs of of *devas* facing each other and holding swords, signifying that the king is surrounded by celestial beings. The thickness of the walls provides another area for decoration around the windows and here these have been painted with trees in Chinese style which probably date to either the Second or Third Reigns, when trading connections with China were at their height and monks.

The four arms of the cruciform plan contain different objects and are used for different functions. Today when ceremonies are held, such as funeral services, the members of the royal family will sit in the southern wing, government officials in the northern wing, the Buddhist monks in the eastern wing and the funeral urn in the western wing. During such occasions the throne and bed described below are used as the altars for Buddha images.

The mother-of-pearl inlaid throne. This stands almost in the centre of the building at the intersection point of the four arms. The throne dates from the beginning of the First Reign and was saved from Phra Thinang Indra Phisek when it burnt down in 1789. The throne is surmounted by a nine-tiered umbrella, symbolising the king's power which extends in eight directions (the four cardinal directions, the four sub-cardinal directions) plus the central direction. The base has five tiers, with mythical creatures guarding the top three tiers: lions and *garudas* on the middle tier, *yakshas* on the next highest tier and *devas* guarding the uppermost tier. The mother-of-pearl inlay is of the highest quality and the throne is a masterpiece of the early Rattanakosin period.

The mother-of-pearl bed. This stands in the eastern arm of the *phra thinang*. It is contemporaneous with the throne and was the bed of King Rama I. Originally it stood in Phra Thinang Phiman Rattaya, but once it was no longer used as a bed it was moved to this location.

Window-style Busabok Mala throne. This half-throne protrudes from the wall in the southern wing of the throne hall behind the mother-of-pearl throne. Its style is similar to the throne in the porch at the front of the building. The base is carved with a row of lions and *garudas* on the lower tier with praying deities above. The throne was constructed during the Fourth Reign so that the ladies of the Inside could see the king while seated behind the lacquerware screen *(see page 126-127)* during the royal ceremonies, keeping them apart from the male members of the royal family.

Below: With increased Chinese influence during the Third Reign, screens would be placed in front of the door as an added protection against evil spirits.

Above: The interior of Phra Thinang Dusit Maha Prasat showing the throne inlaid with mother-of-pearl and surmounted by a nine-tiered white umbrella.

Right: The bed of King Rama I is inlaid with mother-of-pearl. Deities decorate the door panels behind.

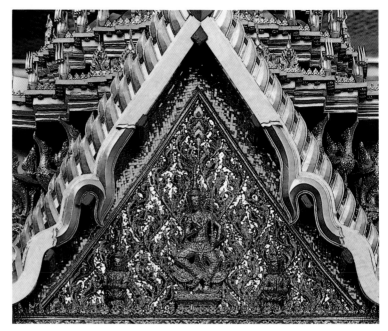

Above: An old photograph showing King Mongkut standing in front of Phra Thinang Aporn Phimok Prasat during the 1865 tonsurate ceremony of Prince Chulalongkorn (later King Rama V) seen here seated on a palanquin. (RBC)

Right: Detail of the pediment of Phra Thinang Aporn Phimok Prasat.

Phra Thinang Aporn Phimok Prasat 34

This small, open pavilion, built to glorify King Rama IV, was constructed on the eastern part of the wall surrounding Phra Thinang Dusit Maha Prasat and was used as a disrobing pavilion by him when processing on palanquin or during the tonsure ceremony. The pavilion is considered to epitomise all the finest qualities of Thai architecture, both in style, proportion and details. A smaller replica was exhibited as part of the Thai exhibit at the Brussels World Fair in 1958.

The pavilion has four porches, of which the northern and southern ones are longer. The roof is topped with a five-tiered spire which means that it is called a *prasat* rather than a *maha prasat*. Where the spire meets the roof, the creatures supporting the spire are swans rather than the more customary *garudas* holding *nagas*. The eastern pediment is carved with Phra Isuan standing on a plinth, one foot raised, holding a sword in his left hand and his right hand raised in blessing. A praying deity flanks him on either side. The redented columns are decorated with gold and silver glass mosaic in a delicate flower pattern and topped with capitals in the form of long-petalled lotuses. Below the pediment hangs another piece of carved wood known in Thai as the *sarai ruang pung* derived from the fact that it looks somewhat as if a bee's nest is attached to the eaves. The sides of this carving run down two-thirds of the columns and terminate in praying deities.

Opposite: Phra Thinang Aporn Phimok Prasat with Phra Thinang Dusit Maha Prasat behind.

Mount Kailasa.

Above: A stone elephant decorating the lower part of Mount Kailasa.

Right: Ho Plueng Krueng.

Ho Plueng Krueng ㉟

This pavilion is situated on the western wall surrounding Phra Thinang Aporn Phimok Prasat. It was constructed during the Sixth Reign for use in a part of the royal funeral rites. It is a two-storey building in traditional Thai style and has a walkway leading to Phra Thinang Dusit Maha Prasat.

Mount Kailasa ㊱

This miniature replica of Mount Kailasa was built during the Fourth Reign as the place where princes and princesses would have a purifying bath during the tonsurate ceremony. On the summit is a miniature palace for Phra Isuan. The lower part is decorated with small animals living in the Himavamsa Forest. Unfortunately the Mount was renovated during the preparations for the Bangkok bicentennial and its original Chinese characteristics have been lost *(see also page 130)*.

Queen Saowabha presiding over a Privy Council Meeting in 1897.

Left: Phra Thinang Rachakaranya Sapha and detail of the pediment showns Phra Narai on garuda.

Phra Thinang Rachakaranya Sapha ㊲

This two-storey building is adjacent to the southern part of the eastern wall of Phra Thinang Aporn Phimok Prasat. King Rama V ordered its construction in order to discuss government affairs with his ministers. In particular, when he made his first trip to Europe in 1897 he installed Queen Saowabha as Regent and she presided over Privy Council Meetings in his stead. In this reign, it has been used once again for Privy Council Meetings and when Her Majesty Queen Sirikit was Regent, while the king entered the monkhood in 1956, she also presided over Privy Council meetings here. Occasionally the king uses the building for private audiences.

The particular characteristics of this building are the pediments which project from the main roof line. This is typical of the Ayutthaya period and is not found anywhere else in the Grand Palace compound. The gilded and glass-mosaic, carved wood pediments show the common motif of Phra Narai on *garuda*. The end windows are unusual in being in a group of three. The interior is decorated entirely in Western style.

The side windows of Phra Thinang Rachakaranya Sapha have double pediments.

You can now stop for a drink or exit by the west door. Alternatively, you can turn right and visit the museum.

Manohra.

Rochana   *Hanuman.*

The Museum of the Emerald Buddha Temple ③⑧

This western-style building was constructed in the Fifth Reign as the Royal Mint. In 1982 for the bi-centennial, the Emerald Buddha Temple was extensively renovated and it was decided that certain architectural elements which had to be replaced should be preserved, together with various artifacts and Buddha images donated to the Emerald Buddha by kings and members of the public. Accordingly HRH Princess Maha Chakri Sirindhorn as Director of the Restoration Committee decided that the Mint should be turned into a museum.

Ground Floor: This floor displays a varied selection of objects associated with the Grand Palace over the centuries. Included are certain elements of Thai architecture, some Buddha images and Chinese stone statues which used to stand in the gardens surrounding the Emerald Buddha Temple. These latter figures represent heros and heroes from Thai literature, such as Ngoh and Rochana from *Sangh Tong* (the Golden Conch), Manohra and Phra Suthon from *Manohra,* Supanmacha and Hanuman from the *Ramakien* and Wimala and Krai Tong from *Krai Tong.* They were carved in the Third Reign and were relocated here to prevent damage.

Thai kings have traditionally been associated with white elephants, which were regarded as extremely auspicious. The more white elephants, the more powerful the king, with King Rama V so far having the greatest number at 19. The bones of

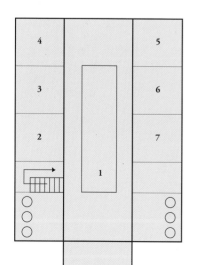

Plan of the ground floor.
No.1 White Elephant Bones.
2-7 Elements of Thai architecture.

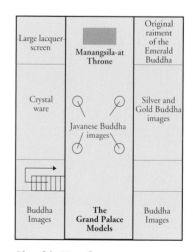

One of the four original Borobudur-style Buddhas moved here from Phra Mondop.

Above left: The Manangsila-at throne which was brought to Bangkok by King Rama IV.

Left: Phra Taen Song Sabai.

previous white elephants are also stored here. The elephants are not actually white, but have certain characteristics such as a pinkish colouring along their spine, or cream surrounds to their eyes and pale toenails.

Also on this floor are ancient cannon which formerly stood on the guard posts of the Grand Palace.

Upper Floor: The first room displays two models of the Grand Palace showing how it was in the First Reign and in this Reign. Behind are a great quantity of Buddha images and commemorative medals created on the occasion of the Bangkok bi-centennial.

In the doorway leading to the main hall is a small mother-of-pearl reclining couch known as the *Phra Taen Song Sabai*. This used to stand in Phra Thinang Phiman Rattaya and the king would use it for informal audiences. It is believed to date from the First Reign.

Large lacquer-screen	Manangsila-at Throne	Original raiment of the Emerald Buddha
Crystal ware	Javanese Buddha images	Silver and Gold Buddha images
Buddha Images	**The Grand Palace Models**	Buddha Images

Plan of the Upper floor.

Below: The magnificent gold and black lacquerware screen.

Opposite
Top: Two views of the Upper Gallery.
Middle right: A miniature of Mount Kailasa made of horns.
Far right: A Chinese-style screen.

In the end of the main hall stands the Manangsila-at throne which is believed to date to the Sukhothai period and was brought to Bangkok by King Rama IV when he was still a monk. Against the walls on either side of the central walkway are four Buddhas in different *mudras* in Javanese style. These used to stand at the corners of the Mondop and were brought from Java by King Chulalongkorn. Off the main hall are four rooms. In the room to the right of the Manangsila-at throne is displayed the original raiments of the Emerald Buddha, together with gold Buddha images and gold betel nut sets. The room opposite displays one enormous gold lacquerware screen showing the coronation of Phra Indra, king of the gods. It was formerly in Phra Thinang Dusit Maha Prasat. It is a masterpiece of Thai lacquerware.

Turning back to the room nearest to the first gallery, the visitor will see a collection of crystal and enamelware presented to the Emerald Buddha. The final gallery displays small Buddha images carved from quartz and ivory, or cast in silver and bronze. These were presented by members of the public.

His Majesty King Bhumibol Adulyadej in full regalia during the Coronation ceremony in 1950.
(Courtesy The Royal Household)

Royal Ceremonies

During the time of the absolute monarchy the buildings that you have visited were the scene of elaborate ceremonies not only for the king, but also his children. Even today the king frequently uses the Grand Palace for important ceremonies such as the Coronation, merit-making, receiving of ambassadors, funeral rites, etc. An significant feature of these ceremonies is that elements of Brahamanism and Buddhism are combined, reflecting a long history which goes back to the time of the Khmer influence before Sukhothai and the adoption of Theravada Buddhism from Sri Lanka. Furthermore while much of the wealth of Ayutthaya was lost, the traditions and rituals were not and it seems that many aspects of Thai ceremonial are little changed since that period.

The buildings which are used for royal ceremonies are Phra Thinang Chakrapat Phiman, Phra Thinang Phaisan Taksin Hall, Phra Thinang Amarin Winichai, the Ubosot of the Emerald Buddha, Phra Thinang Dusit Maha Prasat, Phra Thinang Chakri Maha Prasat. Some of the most important ceremonies provide a fascinating insight into Thai culture, in particular the reverence in which the king is held. The abbrievated descriptions of the ceremonies given below come from the book *'Siamese State Ceremonies'* by H.G. Quaritch Wales, which remains an invaluable reference work. Written over 60 years ago, much of the detail remains the same today, although the Tonsurate Ceremony has not been held since 1932.

King Rama VII prepares to board the Suphanhong Royal Barge to cross to Wat Arun for the Kathin ceremony. (RBC)

Above: The symbolical Mount Kailasa built for the occasion of Tonsurate of HRH Prince Maha Vajirunhis. It was erected on the ground in front of Phra Thinang Chakri Maha Prasat. (RBC)

Right: The procession entering the Grand Palace during the coronation ceremony. Wisetchaisri Gate may be seen in the background. (RBC)

Rites of Passage ceremonies

Various Rites of Passage ceremonies were held for princes of *Chao Fa*, *Phra Ong Chao* and *Mom Chao* rank. The first took place three days after birth and was a small private ceremony orchestrated by Brahmins. The royal baby would lie in the cradle surrounded by important royal princes and princesses, together with ladies-in-waiting of the 'Inside' (that part of the palace reserved for women and children only). The Brahmins entered bearing candles which were then passed from hand to hand around the infant until three circuits had been completed. The Chief Brahmin would then hand the nine coloured threads to the king who would then tie these to the cradle and anoint the child with a special paste. An auspicious time did not need to be sought for this ceremony, which would usually take place in the afternoon or evening.

At one month came a joint Buddhist and Brahmin ceremony. At this point the Royal Astrologer would cast the baby's horoscope. On the eve of the ceremony, Buddhist monks would prepare and bless holy water. On the following day food would be given to the monks in the morning, after which the Brahmin part of the ceremony would begin, with the Brahmin priest blessing a separate bowl of holy water. The three stages of this ceremony then comprised:

     1. cutting a small lock of the baby's hair

     2. naming of the child

     3. circling with candles

Again this ceremony would be performed by the king. After lighting candles and joss sticks in front of the Buddha image, the king would wait while the Brahmin finished preparing the holy water by floating gold and silver prawns and fish and gold and silver coconuts. The Brahmin would then immerse the baby in the water, in a manner reminiscent of a Christian baptism. The king would then pour water over the baby's head and taking the scissors cut his or her hair. The water blessed the previous evening would also be poured over the baby's head, sacred thread was tied around the baby's wrist and paste anointed on his or her head. All the while Buddhist monks would be chanting, the Brahmins blowing their conches and the royal orchestra playing on drums and xylophones. Then the king would present gifts of robes, joss sticks, candles and decorative prayer fans to the Buddhist monks.

Moving to the adjoining room, the naming ceremony now began. As well as receiving a name chosen on the basis of time of birth and horoscope, the prince or princess would be given royal regalia lavishly decorated with gold and including a gold tablet inscribed with the royal name. The Brahmins would hang up the large and ornate cradle below which was spread a mat on which to place the royal offerings of food to the spirits. The king having placed the royal regalia in the cradle, the no-doubt somewhat overawed baby would be lain in the cradle as well. The Brahmins would then rock the cradle, sing to the baby, and blow their conches, while the orchestra played. Finally as in the three-day

Far left: King Rama IV (King Mongkut) standing in front of Phra Thinang Aporn Phimok Prasat during the Tonsurate ceremony of Prince Chulalongkorn in 1865 seen here seated on a palanquin. (RBC)

Middle: HRH Prince Rangsit in ceremonial dress before the top-knot cutting. (Courtesy National Archives)

Above: HRH Princess Hemavadi on the day of her Tonsurate ceremony. (RBC)

HRH Princess Abbhantri Paja in tonsure costume. (RBC)

ceremony, candles were then passed from hand to hand making three circuits of the cradle.

At thirteen to celebrate puberty came the most elaborate ceremony of all – the so-called *Sokan* or Tonsurate Ceremony in which the topknot of hair worn since birth by members of the royal family would be ceremoniously shaved. Spread over a seven-day period the ceremonies are meant to reflect the tonsure ceremony enshrined in Hindu myth of the elephant god Ganesha. For a prince of *Chao Fa* rank, the ceremony would take place on a specially constructed hill of some 20-46 feet in height, echoing the Kailasa hill where the god Shiva is believed to reside. The elaborate design and construction of the stylised hill was rich in symbolic meaning, too complicated to describe here. Equally, space does not allow a full recitation of the rites, but in brief, the ceremonies took the following course. Firstly, auspicious days for the rites were chosen by the Court Astrologer. On the eve of first day holy water was consecrated, sacred thread was tied around the throne hall and Buddhist chanting began. Then on the first day the king, followed by the candidate and the court in brilliant processions and ceremonial dress entered Phra Thinang Dusit Maha Prasat where the ceremony began,

Above: HRH Prince Prajadhipok (later King Rama VII) after the Tonsurate. (RBC)

Right: HRH Prince Chudadhuj receiving some auspicious water from the Brahmin while King Rama V looks on. (RBC)

accompanied by a cacophany of sound from the orchestra, drums and gongs. The actual Tonsurate Ceremony took place in Phra Thinang Dusit Maha Prasat on the fourth day, while the fifth and sixth days were devoted to propititation of the *kwan* or spirits, 22 of which are traditionally believed to inhabit the human form and protect the human from harm. Finally on the seventh day the hair, enclosed in a small bag and placed in a casket, would be floated away borne in state on a royal barge on the Chao Phraya river. Once opposite the Temple of the Dawn (Wat Arun), the casket would be consigned to the river.

An official picture of HRH Prince Prajadhipok in full dress with Krom Khun rank regalia. (RBC)

Throughout this week of ceremonies for the tonsuarate, entertainments were laid on for courtiers and members of the general public to enjoy. These included acrobats performing on bamboo poles, so-called Annamite vaulters who turned somersaults and did various tumbling tricks, Malay performers who lay on sharp weapons, sword tossing, a Chinese dragon dance and a buffalo pantomime, the latter said to originate in Burma. Dancing girls and actors performed plays and dances later on in the week and singers entertained the onlookers at various times. All in all, the Tonsurate Ceremony was an opportunity for great celebration and show, combining elements from Buddhism, Brahminism and animism, as well as dances and plays from other countries of Southeast Asia, India and China, reflecting Thailand's position at a crossroads of cultural influences. Accounts by foreign visitors to Siam in the seventeenth century mention the performances of such dances and plays at royal ceremonies in Ayutthaya, and doubtless some date back even earlier.

The last Tonsurate was performed on 29th March 1932. The revolution which transformed Siam from an absolute to a constitutional monarchy occurred only three months later. An era in which lavish and elaborate ceremonies were held to celebrate the important events of royal lives was to end for ever. Thus while magnificent ceremonies are still held today, unlike in the reigns of King Mongkut and King Chulalongkorn when Rites of Passage ceremonies were performed for the many royal children, today all the ceremonies are of shorter duration and are confined to the King, the Queen and their immediate family. The accompanying entertainments of acrobats, dancers, sword fighting and plays are no more – sadly, they no longer have a place in the busy and competitive world of modern Thailand.

HH Princess Suddhasiri Sobha on the day of her Tonsurate, 29 March 1932. This was the last occasion on which the tonsurate ceremony was ever performed. (Courtesy M.R. Sunida Kitiyakara)

King Prajadhipok (King Rama VII) in white bathing robe within the special bathing pavilion.(RBC)

The Coronation

For three days before the actual day of crowning, the Court Brahmins performed sacrifices to Fire in a ceremonial pavilion specially erected near Phra Thinang Amarin Winichai, in which nine basins of water were purified by the recitation of specific texts. Leaves from certain medicinal trees were steeped in the water and sent to the king, while others were dipped in honey and oil and placed in the fire. At the beginning of these ceremonies offerings were also made to the Hindu deities in the Brahmin temples, before the royal white umbrellas and before the images of the city guardians.

Simultaneously with the Brahmin ceremonies, Buddhist services took place in all the sections of the royal residence and protective thread was stretched around the buildings. Each evening a high-ranking monk delivered a sermon in Phra Thinang Phaisan Thaksin, with the king in partial attendance and the following morning the king presented food to the officiating monks.

The Ceremonial bath

On the morning of the actual day the king proceeded to Phra Thinang Phaisan Thaksin where princes, foreign representatives and high officials were waiting. After making his profession of the Buddhist faith, the Chief Brahmin invited him to take a ceremonial bath of purification and anointment. This bath took place in a special pavilion situated between Phra Thinang Phaisan Thaksin and Phra Thinang Chakrapat Phiman (such ablution pavilions probably date back to ancient Indian tradition). The water used in the ceremony originated from the five principal rivers of the kingdom (the Chao Phraya, the Pasak, the Rajburi, the Petchaburi and Bang Pakong); from the four ponds at Supanburi (used in such ceremonies from the period of Ayutthaya onwards) and some of the water consecrated by monks from every province of the country.

The king being seated in the pavilion, some water was handed to him by a Brahmin in a small golden bowl,

Left: King Prajadhipok sitting on the Octagonal Throne, Phra Thinang Atthathit. (RBC)

Above: King Prajudhipok seated on the Bhadrabitha throne before receiving the royal regalia from the Brahmans and Pandits. (RBC)

King Prajadhipok seated on the Bhadrabitha Throne after having received the royal regalia. (RBC)

which the king dipped his hand and rubbed the water on the top of his head. By pulling a rope a shower was then released from the canopy above through the petals of a golden lotus thereby signifying the celeslial nature of the shower. Finally ministers and elder relatives poured water over the kings hands. While the ceremonial bath was in progress, ancient guns were fired within the precincts of the palace, a fanfare of drums and trumpets was sounded, and the Brahmins played their ceremonial music, while 80 Buddhist monks chanted stanzas of benediction.

After the ceremonial bath the king retired and reappeared in full regalia before making his way to Phra Thinang Phaisan Thaksin preceded by Brahmins and the Court Pandits bearing images of Ganesha and the Buddha image of Phra Chai Lang Chang *(see page 55)*. Other Brahmins played drums and blew conches, while another scattered roasted grains of rice.

On entering the *phra thinang* the king seated himself on the Octagonal Throne *(see pages 98 and 135)* beneath the seven-tiered white umbrella. Opposite each face of the throne stood a small table bearing an image of the guardian of that particular

King Prajadhipok in full state robes and wearing Katin Crown anoints Queen Rambhai Barni during her Installation. (RBC)

direction *(lokapala)* and the ceremonial water and conch. Beginning with the east, the direction in which the king faces, the Pandit for this point advances and hands the king a conch for him to anoint himself while offering a blessing relating to the eastern region. Next comes the direction of the south-east and so on in a clockwise with the king turning to face each Pandit in turn. After each blessing the king promises to protect the kingdom, its Buddhist religion and its people.

The Ceremony on the Octagonal Throne having been completed the king moves to the western part of Phra Thinang Phaisan Thaksin, preceded by the Brahmins and Pandits and followed by chamberlains and pages bearing the royal regalia of the Great White Umbrella of State, the Sceptre, the Fan, the Stick, the Receptacle, the Brahman Girdle, the Girdle of Brilliants, the Whisk of the Yak's Tail, the Diamond Ring, the Betel Nut Set, the Golden Tablet of Style and Title, the Girdle of the Nine Gems, the Whisk of the White Elephant's Tail, the Ring, the Water Urn, the Great Crown of Victory, the Sword of Victory, the Slippers, the Personal Sword, and the Libation Vessel. There follows also the Eight Weapons of Sovereignty comprising the

One of the royal barges, Ananta Nagaraja, in the Royal Procession by water. (RBC)

Hostage Sword, the Long-Handled Sword, the Discus, the Sword and Buckler, the Trident, the Bow, the Diamond Spear, the Gun of the Satong.

The actual coronation takes place on the Bhadrabitha throne, which before the coronation is surmounted with a seven-tiered umbrella, and afterwards with a nine-tiered one. The Chief Brahmin then comes before the king and, after rendering homage, makes a speech first in Tamil, then in Pali and finally in Thai, at the same time handing the king the Golden Tablet of Style and Title. The High Priest of Shiva then takes the Great Crown of Victory and hands it to the king who puts it on his own head, accompanied by Brahmanic music and fanfare, the firing of salutes and ringing of monastery bells throughout the country. One by one other items of the regalia are handed to the king who touches them to signify his acceptance. The Brahmins then give a final benediction. Being fully crowned, the king scatters gold and silver flowers and coins among the Brahmins, a gesture repeated later outside. As Quaritch Wales has pointed out, the symbolism throughout the ceremony is based on the assumption that the chief deities, particularly Phra Isuan, are invited down to earth to become merged in the person of the crowned king, a milder version of the *devaraja* cult prevalent in earlier times in Cambodia.

After the crowning, the king then removes the crown once more in order to go to Phra Thinang Chakrapat Phiman, with chamberlains and pages bearing the regalia in order to receive the blessing from the Supreme Patriarch and the assembled senior monks.

Next follows an audience in Phra Thinang Amarin Winichai to receive homage from the royal family and officials. Here the king is seated on the Phra Thinang Phuthan Tong throne and a senior member of the royal family reads an address of congratulation. After this general audience the king then dons another crown, the Kathin crown, and retires to Phra Thinang Phaisan Thaksin for the Queen's investiture and to receive the congratulations of the ladies.

Then in the afternoon, the king wearing the Great Crown is carried on a palanquin to the Temple of the Emerald Buddha. Before entering he removes the crown to don a Royal Hat. In the Ubosot he makes offerings of gold and silver flowers and lights candles before declaring his willingness to become 'defender of the Buddhist faith'.

Finally, again on a palanquin and wearing the Great Crown, the king proceeds to Phra Thinang Dusit Maha Prasat. Outside he dismounts, removes the crown and enters to pay homage to the memory of his predecessors.

On the following two days more audiences were held for the special envoys of foreign powers and officials.

King Prajadhipok seated on the palanquin after changing his robes in Phra Thinang Dusidaphirom to join the royal procession by land to the Temple of the Emerald Buddha. (RBC)

The Great Crown of Victory. (By Royal Permission)

Siamese Royal Regalia

Royal regalia has come to be seen as essential adjuncts of the king and like the accompanying ceremonial serves to impress the people with the respect due to the king.

Five items among the regalia are undoubtedly of great antiquity and date back to early Indian history: the Great White Umbrella of State, the Great Crown of Victory, the Sword of Victory, the Slippers, the Fan.

The Great White Umbrella of State: These tiered umbrellas exist in four levels: three tiers, five tiers, seven for the king before he is fully crowned and nine thereafter. Similar umbrellas are found in Cambodia and Burma, appear in the reliefs of Borobodur in Java and Angkor Wat, as well as in Indian literature of an even earlier date. Indeed, in ancient India it seems that the umbrella was of far greater importance than the crown itself. It is even possible that its origins can be traced back to Egyptian times. The greater the number of tiers the greater the honour accorded.

The Great Crown of Victory: The Thai *mongkut* may be likened to a cone of several stages terminating in a tapering spire. This particular crown was created by King Rama I for his second coronation ceremony in 1785. It has been used in the coronation by every king since that time. The whole crown is highly ornamented and is surmounted by a minute, tapering umbrella. The modern Cambodian crown has the same form as the Thai. Perhaps the form evolved from the adaptation of a protective helmet and also the particular hair style worn by the Thai troops as shown on the reliefs of Angkor Wat. In addition, Quaritch Wales suggests that the high, tapering top is influenced by the finials associated with the Buddhist flame-shaped finial, originally derived from Sri Lanka. In contrast, the Royal Hats, worn when going to and from particular ceremonies are known to be of European

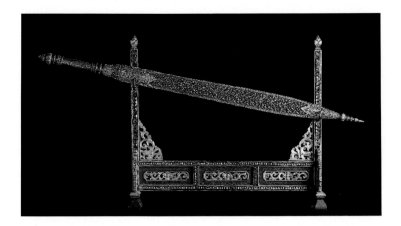

origin, being derived from the court of Louis XIV in the seventeenth century.

The Sword of Victory: One of the foremost among royal regalia, the blade of this sword was brought from Cambodia in 1783. King Rama I ordered the creation of a new golden handle and scabbard. It was also used in the 1785 Coronation and is believed to be an emblem of ancient Khmer sovereignty, perhaps dating to the 10th century. The Khmers must, in turn, have derived their idea of a Sacred Sword from India, where it is mentioned in the *Mahavamsa*.

The Slippers: In ancient Thailand, as in Cambodia, shoes were probably regarded as suitable only for royalty and may even have been considered as having magical properties. Made from gold they are only used during the coronation ceremony. According to HSH Princess Poonpismai Diskul they are exremely heavy.

The Fan: This is the last item of the regalia that may be shown to have links with ancient India. Again its Cambodian origin may be seen from its appearance on the reliefs of Angkor Wat. The fan, as a royal adjunct, is associated with the idea of coolness and sublime comfort attributed to divine kings, a particularly attractive quality in hot countries. This fan was created in the reign of King Rama I and, known in Thai as *'Valavichinee'*, is linked with the Royal Whisks, both being associated with a waving motion.

The Whisks from Yak's and White Elephants tails: The former is a very ancient emblem which seems on occasion to have replaced the fan in importance, being associated with kings from the time of ancient India. Whisks also frequently appear on the bas-reliefs of Angkor and Borobodur. The White Elephant's Tail Whisk was created in the First Reign.

The Stick. (By Royal Permission).

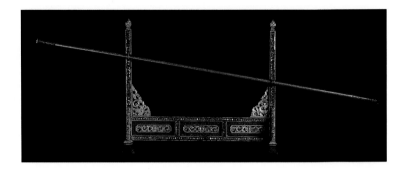

The Sceptre and Stick: These seem to be two forms of the same emblem and do not appear in Indian literature. The form is similar to that used by monks during funeral ceremonies, having a pointed top and a three-pronged point. It was created by King Rama I and could be used to jab into the ground to prevent slipping. It has, however, never been used in this way.

The Personal Sword: This may correspond to the golden sword to which Chou Ta-Kuan makes mention during his trip to Angkor in 1295. Apparently this sword was worn by the king whenever he left his palace.

The Brahmin Girdle: This traditional attribute of Phra Isuan reinforces the concept of the god merging with the king.

The other Girdles and Rings: Formerly these were probably amulets, in particular the Girdle of the Nine Gems, symbolizing the planets. Once again similar ornaments were worn by the Khmer kings, as well as being mentioned in the *Jatakas* and the *Ramayana*.

The Receptacle, the Betel Nut Set, the Water Urn and Libation Vessel: Such items of personal use became associated in Indo-China with insignia of rank not only for the king but for officials to whom similar articles were presented by the king when they received promotion. Yet again the Angkor reliefs show similar articles.

The Golden Tablets of Style and Title: This is an extremely important item of the regalia and considerable preparation is involved, with the special inscription ceremony being preceded by Buddhist prayers of benediction and then attended by Buddhist monks at a time determined by the royal astrologer, some three weeks before the coronation. While one scribe engraved the king's name, another inscribed the Royal Horoscope on another gold plate while monks recited prayers and Brahmins

The Slippers. (By Royal Permission)
Above left: The Whisk and the Fan. (By Royal Permission)

blew the conches and played other ceremonial instruments. The plates were then anointed with lustral water from conches. The two gold plates are then rolled up in red silk and placed in a gold tube, within a golden box, which in turn is placed on a two-tiered gold plate, upon a gold stand. The gold box is then housed in the Ubosot until the day before the coronation when, with the other regalia, it is carried on a palanquin to Phra Thinang Phaisan Thaksin.

The custom of kings changing their names upon accession to the throne seems to have been common throughout the countries influenced by Indian culture and beliefs, as may be seen in Cambodia where the king customarily took the suffix of -*varman* upon ascending the throne, or in Pagan and elsewhere in Burma and in Sukhothai, culminating in the extremely long Sanskrit ephithets enjoyed by Siamese kings in the Ayutthaya period.

The Eight Weapons of Sovereignty: The bow may be the oldest article surviving from Indian regalia, while the Trident and Discus are attributes of Phra Isuan and Phra Narai and symbolize the king's identification with these gods. The other weapons appear to be of purely Siamese origin and seem to be connected with King Naresuan (r. 1590-1610).

After the coronation ceremonies within the Grand Palace, two Coronation processions take place within the capital: one through the streets on the royal palanquin and one by barge down the Chao Phraya river. During these the monarch visits various temples and the general populace have a chance to see him. Undoubtedly the royal barge procession is one of the most memorable Thai ceremonies and the most recent occurrence was on the occasion of the 50th anniversary of His Majesty King Bhumibol Adulyadej's accession to the throne.

The lying-in-state of the Late Queen Saowabha on the western wing in Phra Thinang Dusit Maha Prasat in 1919. (RBC)

Cremation

Cremation is the sole means of disposal of deceased royalty in Thailand and for Thai Buddhists in general. However, in comparison to the cremation of an ordinary person, that of a royal person of high rank, or especially the king, is distinguished by its great length and elaborate ceremonial. Kings are generally not cremated until many months after their death. Although various details of the ceremonies have changed there is no doubt that the cremation and pre-cremation rites are closely based on practices dating from the Ayutthaya period. It should also be noted that Thai cremation ceremonies, while in accordance with Buddhist principles, also embody many Brahmanical elements, which, as with other ceremonial features we have encountered, came to Siam via Cambodia.

Once the king is dead, the royal princes approach and place him on his back, closing the eyes and mouth, and covering the body with a golden shroud. The new king is then confirmed and the princes return and bathe the corpse with scented water. The body is then prepared for the Urn, being dressed with special clothes and gold ornaments. In particular a gold mask covers the face, symbolic of the radiant visage of a god. A pair of gilt candles, a lotus, and a pair of gold horns, containing areca nut wrapped in betel leaf, are placed in the hands, while a silken hat is placed on his head. The body is then placed inside two urns: the inner of silver is hermetically sealable, while the outer of gold is elaborately ornamented. In order to fit into the urn, the corpse has to be secured into a sitting position with the knees bent. The late king's personal Kathin Crown is placed upon his head by the new king and a diamond-studded gold chain hung around his

neck. The corpse is saluted by all present and then fitted into the inner urn, before being placed in the outer urn and moved under a nine-tiered Umbrella of State from Phra Thinang Chakrapat Phiman to Phra Thinang Dusit Maha Prasat, preceded by the usual drummers, processional umbrella-bearers and Brahmins playing ceremonial instruments. Within Phra Thinang Dusit the Urn is placed in the west wing on the royal catafalque, being slowly drawn up a slope accompanied by the blowing of conches and firing of guns. Throughout the 'sitting-in-state' the Urn is surmounted by a nine-tiered umbrella and is constantly guarded by a military guard, while daily ceremonies are conducted in which Buddhist monks sustain almost constant chanting. Those entering the Phra Thinang to participate in prayers pay homage to the Urn by prostrating themselves. Special religious services are held on the seventh, fiftieth and hundredth days after death. On these days Chinese and Annamite monks also perform special ceremonies outside. In front of their altar are placed elaborate paper models of household items, vehicles, etc. These are burnt following the cremation according to ancient Chinese tradition whereby such models symbolize the objects that the deceased will need in his next life. While the lying-in-state takes place the depositions of the body can pass from the inner urn through a grating in its base to be collected in a vessel and taken to Wat Mahathat where they are mixed with dry sugar cane and incense before being burned and then kept to be mixed with the ashes after the cremation. Also during this time the sacred fire to be used in the cremation is kept burning on an altar in Phra Thinang Dusit.

Above left and right: The paper models of household items. (RBC)

The court officers prepare King Rama V's Royal Urn on the palanquin after being moved from Phra Thinang Dusit Maha Prasat, while the new king, King Rama VI and his mother, Queen Saowabha look on prior to the procession to Sanam Luang. (RBC)

The funeral pyre: Soon after the death of the late king, work begins at Sanam Luang on the construction of the funeral pyre, or Phra Meru, symbolizing Mount Meru, the home of the gods.

The structure must be made from all new materials which can never again be used for a similar purpose. Surrounding the Meru must also be constructed pavilions for important officials, members of the royal family and the most important pavilion for the king. Recently for the cremation of the Princess Mother, the Meru was 37.20 m high and was constructed of wood.

Stages in the Cremation: On the morning of the Cremation Day, immediately after the last Buddhist service, the Urn is lifted down from the catafalque, the Outer Urn is removed and the inner one opened so the crown and other gold ornaments can be removed from the body. The bones are then replaced in the Inner Urn, with the Outer Urn around it and borne on a palanquin in a procession to Wat Chetuphon (Wat Pho). During the procession those steadying the urn must be sons or nephews of the king with the rank of *Mom Chao* or above. Having circled Wat Pho, the procession wends its way back to Sanam Luang where it is met by the Grand Funeral Procession and the Urn is

transferred to the Great Funeral Carriage, a most magnificent carved, gilded and bejewelled boat-shaped throne. Another similar throne transports the Supreme Patriarch to Sanam Luang and precedes the Urn. Formerly, in a tradition which has now been abolished, a procession of mythical animals preceded by an effigy of a rhinoceros bearing the 'sacred fire'.

Upon reaching the Meru the Urn is transferred to a gun carriage or palanquin and the procession then circumambulates the Meru three times counter-clockwise, the direction reserved for inauspicious occasions. The procession halts at the eastern stairway of the Meru so the Inner Urn, the outer one now removed, can be hoisted up the inclined plane to the top of the Meru. The king then ascends the Meru by the western staircase and pays hommage to the remains. Formerly the Urn would remain *in situ* for about 15 days, but, since the 1920s, cremation has taken place on the same day. The Inner Urn is now replaced

Top Left and right: The Royal Urn being tranferred to the Great Funeral Carriage by the manual elevator. (RBC)

The procession carrying the remains of King Rama V in the Royal Great Urn to the Royal Pyre at Sanam Luang in 1911. (RBC)

Above: The small Urn containing the bone relics has been placed on the Royal Catafalque in Phra Thinang Dusit Maha Prasat for special religious services. (RBC)

Top left: The Royal Cremation ceremony of King Rama V at Sanam Luang. (RBC)

Top right: The funeral pyre of King Rama IV was one of the biggest and highest in the Rattanakosin period.

by one of sandalwood. The king and queen return at around 4 in the afternoon and shortly afterwards the king ascends the stairway to apply the sacred fire. After them a long procession of government officials and members of the royal family ascend to add their offerings of candles and sandlewood. The pyre continues to burn all night under the watchful eye of attendants.

On the following day consecrated water is poured on the hot ashes and small fragments of bone, in analogy to the miraculous shower of rain that extinguished the Buddha's pyre. More rites are then performed by the monks in attendance and the gifts of robes and food made by the king are circumambulated three times around the Meru in a clockwise direction. The king, queen and children search through the ashes for small bone relics, to distribute to children if appropriate. However at the cremation of King Rama VI all the relics were perfumed and placed in a small golden urn some 50 cm high and carried in state to the Grand Palace where they remain. The ashes, fragments of burnt wood, etc, are enshrined in various temples in Bangkok built during the reign of that particular monarch. Thus those of King Rama I are in Wat Pho; King Rama II in Wat Arun; King Rama III in Wat Ratchaorot; King Rama IV in Wat Ratchapradit and King Rama V in Wat Benjamabhopit. There are no Bangkok temples associated specifically with the reigns of Kings Rama VI-VIII. The ashes of King Rama VI are underneath the Standing Buddha outside the Phra Pathom Chedi in Nakhon Pathom Province. Those of King Rama VII are interred at Wat Ratchabhopit. King Rama VIII's ashes are at Wat Suthat, the temple where he proclaimed his adherence to and protection of Buddhism.

Opposite: The Royal Urn on its circumambulation of the Royal Pyre prior to the cremation of King Rama V in 1911. (RBC)

The Kings of the Chakri Dynasty

Absolute Monarchy

King Rama I (King Phra Buddha Yodfa Chulalok)	1782-1809	The Grand Palace complex Emerald Buddha Temple The outer wall and forts Phra Thinang Dusit Maha Prasat Phra Thinang Phiman Rattaya Phra Thinang Chakrapat Phiman Phra Thinang Phaisan Thaksin Phra Thinang Amarin Winichai Phra Thinang Dusidaphirom Ho Phra That Monthien Ho Phra Sulalai Piman Two Golden Chedis Ho Phra Nak The Belfry
King Rama II (King Phra Buddha Lertla Naphalai)	1809-1824	Phra Thinang Sanam Chan Suan Kwa
King Rama III (King Nang Klao)	1824-1851	Phra Thinang Sutthai Sawan Prasat Row of the 8 prangs Viharn Yod
King Rama IV (King Mongkut)	1851-1868	Phra Thinang Mahisorn Prasat Phra Thinang Aporn Phimok Prasat Prasat Phra Thep Bidorn Phra Sri Rattana Chedi Buddha Viham Gandhara Phra Buddha Rattanasathan Phra Photithat Piman Ho Rajakoramanusorn Ho Rajabongsanusorn
King Rama V (King Chulalongkorn)	1868-1910	The Chakri Maha Prasat Group Phra Thinang Sivalai Maha Prasat Phra Thinang Boromphiman Phra Thinang Ratchakaranya Sapha
King Rama VI (King Vajiravudh)	1910-1925	Sitaraphirom Pavilion Racharuedee Pavilion
King Rama VII (King Prajadhipok) Revolution	1925-1935 1932	No building but renovation for 150 year celebrations

Constitutional Monarchy

King Rama VIII (King Ananda Mahidol)	1935-1946	
King Rama IX (King Bhumibol Adulyadej)	1946	1982 Bangkok bi-centennial renovation.

THE CHAKRI DYNASTY

King Rama I.

King Rama II.

King Rama III.

King Rama IV.

King Rama V.

King Rama VI.

King Rama VII.

King Rama VIII.

King Rama IX.

Style of doors and windows used in the Grand Palace.

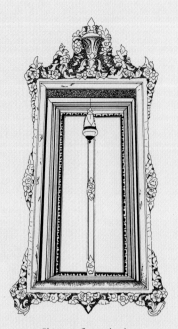

Chinese-influenced style

Thai traditional style

Mongkut style

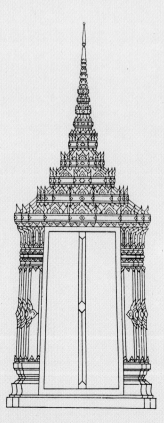

Mondop style

1 hornlike finial on the roof ridge, representing the head of the *garuda. (Chofa)*

2 toothlike ridges on the sloping edges of a gable, representing the fin on the back of the *naga. (Bairaka)*

3 main purlin, central purlin. *(Paelan)*

4 gable beam. *(Krajang)*

5 sloping edges of the naga. *(Lamyong)*

6 small finials jutting out of the 2 corners of the gable, representing the heads of the *naga. (Hang Hong)*

7 niche. *(Pang Kong Song)*

8 column purlin. *(Pae Huasao)*

9 decorative panel for covering hidden structure. *(Bang Nok)*

10 eave. *(Cheing Klon)*

11 lotus capital pillar. *(Bua Huasao)*

12 space-filler. *(Tin Phi)*

13 underside structure of the eaves. *(Saphan Nu)*

14 cantilever beam. *(Tao Rai)*

15 purlin at the end of cantilever beam. *(Pae Plaitao)*

16 decorative.

17 eaves brackets. *(Kuantuay)*

18 fillet. *(Puke)*

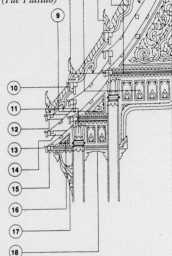

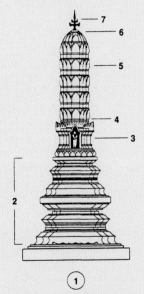

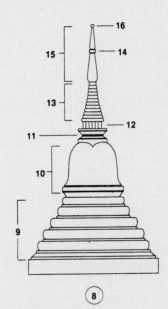

1-7 **prang (a Khmer-style cornshaped chedi/stupa)**

2 superimposed lion-footed pedestals 3. niches on four sides

4 lotus amulet

5 leaf-like lotus petal decorative element

6 apex

7 Shiva's weapon: multi-pronged metal spire on top of a prang

8-16 circular chedi or stupa (in Lankan bell shape)

9 superimposed circular pedestals

10 bell-shaped form; body of the chedi

11 square form representing a throne

12 small columns, balusters

13 layers of receding circular mouldings on top of a chedi

14 amulet

15 circular tapering finial

16 topmost orb

17-24 squared-based chedi with indented corners

18 superimposed lion-footed pedestals

19 lotus moulding

20 indented bell-shaped form; body of the stupa

21 indented square form representing a throne

22 layers of receding lotus mouldings

23 tapering finial

24 topmost orb

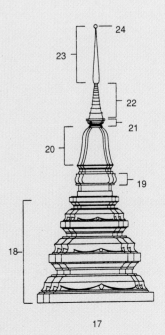

Glossary

bairaka Toothlike ridges on the sloping edges of the roof gable, see p. 154.

bikshuni Buddhist nuns.

Bodhisattva In Mahayana Buddhism, one who is able to reach nirvana but delays doing so in order to help other suffering beings.

Brahma One of the three main Hindu gods. He is usually depicted with four arms and four heads and may be mounted on his vehicle a *hong* (hamsa).

Brahmins Hindu Priests who participate and officiate at many ceremonies in the Grand Palace.

busabok An open carved and gilded throne with a tapering roof with spire.

Chao Fa A child born to the king and a queen. The highest level of prince or princess.

chedi A Buddhist building with spire, housing a relic of the Buddha, a king or a prince, see p. 154.

chofa Roof finial on the roof ridge, see p. 154.

deva A god or goddess, or a celestial creature inhabiting the lower levels of Buddhist heaven. Appears in Thai iconography as a guardian of important buildings.

devaraja Divine king.

Erawan The three-headed elephant mount of Indra, known in India as Airavata.

Ganesha The elephant-headed son of Shiva.

garuda A half-man half-bird mythological figure, the mount of Phra Narai (Vishnu). Widely used in architecture, particularly on pediments, of royal buildings.

Himavamsa Forest The mythical forest around Mount Sumeru.

hamsa Sacred goose and mount of Brahma.

hang hong The finials on Thai temples and kingly palaces at the lower edge of the roof.

Ho A hall.

hong A swan.

Indra The Vedic god of the sky, clouds and monsoon and guardian of the east. His mount is the three-headed elephant Erawan.

kanok A common Thai design, see p. 154.

kathin ceremony A ceremony in which the king presents new robes to the monks at the end of their rains retreat in around October or November.

khao A mountain.

kratong A container made from banana leaves and flowers, used to present offerings to Buddha images or relics.

lokapala The saviours of the world and guardians of the various compass points.

Maharat The great, usually applied to a king.

Mahayana Buddhism According to this 'Great Vehicle' of Buddhism, the historical Buddha is one of many Bodhisattvas and Buddhas who have gained enlightenment.

makara A scaly sea monster who is half-crocodile, half-elephant.

Mom Chao A prince or princess born of a male Chao Fa or male Phra Ong Chao prince and an ordinary woman.

mondop The Thai word for *mandapa*; a Thai-style building with seven-tiered spire.

Mount Phra Sumeru The cosmic, or World Mountain of Hindu cosmology which lies at the centre of the universe and is the abode of the gods. Both the spire of *Phra Maha Prasats* and the base of thrones are symbolic representations of this mountain, so that the king is thus equated with a divine being.

muang City, or town.

naga A water serpent with many mythological associations – fertility, rainbows and creation. Widely used in architecture, particularly on the roofs and superstructures of Thai-style buildings, as a guardian figure.

Phra Maha Monthien A royal residence, whose multi-tiered roof and elevated floor signified the honour of the king.

Phra Maha Prasat A Thai-style building with a seven-tiered spire, constructed to glorify and symbolize the divinity of the king with many specific symbolic architectural elements.

Phra Narai Known in India as Vishnu. One of the three main Hindu deities, worshipped as the preserver and protector. The king is linked symbolically with Vishnu, hence the common appearance of Vishnu on pediments of important royal buildings.

Phra Thinang A throne hall, or used more generally for buildings used by the king and the highest level princes.

prang A stepped type of *chedi* with corn-cob shaped spire, derived from Khmer architecture.

prasat A building designed to illustrate the importance of the king. Similar but less important than a *Phra Maha Prasat*, having a five-tiered spire.

Ramakien The Thai version of the Indian *Ramayana* epic, see p. 30.

Rattanakosin One of the names for Bangkok.

Rattanakosin period The period dating from 1782 to the present. Often used in connection with art and architecture.

sala A pavilion.

sanam Ground or field.

sema stones The stones around an *ubosot* to define the confines of the sacred area in which Buddhist monks could be ordained.

singha A lion, which is often used in architecture as a guardian.

suan A garden.

tamnak A princely residence, or palace.

thanon A road.

Theravada Buddhism The so-called 'lesser vehicle' of Buddhism which spread to Southeast Asia to Sri Lanka. It concentrates on the textual doctrine of the historical Buddha rather than the pantheon of Bodhisattvas of Mahayana Buddhism.

thep chumnum Assembly of the deities, a scene frequently portrayed in temple murals during the Ayutthaya period but uncommon later.

theppanom Deities kneeling in a praying posture.

tim Various meanings a soldier's barracks standing against the palace wall; a Thai-style pavilion used by high ranking officials waiting to see the king; a pavilion for Buddhist monks.

Traiphum 'The Three Worlds' of heaven, earth and hell, of Buddhist cosmology. It is the title of a Buddhist treatise allegedly written by King Lithai. It was revised by King Rama I.

Tripitaka The 'Three Baskets' of the Buddhist canon: the Vinaya (the rules), the Suttanta (the Buddha's discourses) and the Abhidhamma (the metaphysical treatises).

viharn A Buddhist building within the temple complex used for various ceremonies apart from ordination of monks.

viman A tri-partite pavilion, the emblem of King Rama III.

wang A palace.

Wang Lang The Rear Palace of the Second Deputy King.

Wang Luang The palace of the king.

Wang Na The Front Palace of the Deputy King.

wat A temple.

yaksha A giant demon.

Further Reading

Beck, Steve Van, *Bangkok Only Yesterday*, Hong Kong: Hong Kong Publishing Co. Ltd, 1982.

Ed. Chakrabongse, Narisa, *A Pictorial Record of the Fifth Reign*, Bangkok: River Books, 1993.

Chula Chakrabongse, HRH Prince, *Lords of Life*, Bangkok: DD Books, 1982.

Finestone, Jeffrey, *The Royal Family of Thailand – The Descendants of King Chulalongkorn*, Bangkok: Phitsanulok Publishing, 1989.

Hunter, Eileen with Chakrabongse, Narisa, *Katya & the Prince of Siam*, Bangkok: River Books, 1994.

Leonowens, A. H., *An English Governess at the Siamese Court*, Singapore: Oxford University Press, 1990.

Smithies, Michael, *Old Bangkok,* Singapore: Oxford University Press, 1986.

Pramoj, M. R. Kukrit, *Si Phaendin* (Four Reigns), Bangkok: Duang Kamol, 1982.

Sternstein, Larry, *Portrait of Bangkok*, Bangkok: Bangkok Metropolitan Administration, 1982.

Suksri, M.R. Naengnoi, *Palaces of Bangkok – the Royal Residences of the Chakri Dynasty*, Bangkok: River Books, 1996.

Warren, William, *The Grand Palace*, Bangkok: The Office of His Majesty's Principal Private Secretary, 1988.

Wyatt, David, *Thailand: A Short History*, London: Yale University Press, 1984.

Practical Information

The Grand Palace is situated in the heart of Old Bangkok and it is possible to combine your visit with one or more of the sites listed below, whose location is given on the map on page 10. Opening times and directions are given under each heading.

The Grand Palace

Open: seven days a week from 8.30-16.00. Last admission is 15.30. The admission charge is 125 baht for foreigners. Shorts and flip flops are not permitted, but sarongs are available at the entrance. Occasionally, special events or ceremonies may restrict access.

Transport:

Buses nos. 1, 2, 3, 6, 15, 19, 25, 30, 32, 33, 43, 44, 47, 53, 60, 64, 65, 70, 80, 82, 91, 123 and Air Bus nos. 5, 6, 7, 8, 12, 36, 44, 80, 91 stop at Sanam Luang in front of the Grand Palace. The express boat pier nearest to the Grand Palace is Ta Chang Pier.

A Tuk-Tuk tram for tourists runs from here to other sites listed below on Fridays, Saturdays and Sundays.

The National Museum

Housed in what was formerly the palace of the Deputy Kings, the museum displays a comprehensive collection of Thai art, sculpture, precious objects, and numerous items from the decorative arts.

Open: Wednesday - Sunday from 9.00-16.00. Admission charge: 40 baht.

Transport: As above. The Museum is a short stroll from the Grand Palace.

Wat Mahathat

This was formerly the temple of the Front Palace and was built by the Deputy King of King Rama I. All the major cities of Thailand traditionally have a Wat Mahathat. The Ubosot is particularly worth seeing.

Open: daily from 7.00-17.30. Admission is free.

The National Gallery

Contains a collection of contemporary art. Temporary exhibitions are sometimes held.

Open: Wednesday - Sunday from 9.00-16.00.

Admission charge: 30 baht.

Transport: as above. The National Gallery is at the northern end of Sanam Luang.

The National Theatre

At certain times productions of Thai Khon (masked dance dramas from the Ramakien and other Thai classics) are performed here. Currently under restoration and will be reopened in 2000.

Wat Arun

Just across the river from the Grand Palace, the tall *prang* of this temple in Khmer-revival style must be one of Bangkok's most distinctive landmarks. Visitors can easily take a short boat trip across the Chao Phraya river from Ta Chang Pier shown on the map.

Open: daily from 7.30-17.00.

Admission charge: 10 baht.

Wat Pho

About 10 minutes walk south of the Grand Palace is Wat Chetuphon, popularly known as Wat Pho. Well-known for the enormous reclining Buddha image, the temple is full of interest, as well as being the home of a Thai tradional massage school, where visitors may enjoy a massage for around 200 baht.

Open: daily from 8.00-17.00. The entrance for foreign tourists is on Chetuphon Road.

Admission charge: 20 baht.

Further afield visitors may stroll around Chinatown, or the Flower Market of Pak Klong Talad. The latter is particularly active in the evening, when as well as the flower market cheap clothes are sold from stalls surrounding the foot of Memorial Bridge. Avoid the flower market on Wednesdays because footpath selling is prohibited for cleaning.

Restaurants

There are numerous riverside restaurants situated off Maharaj Road which runs parallel to the river behind Wat Mahathat.

Index